—THE LOST— FREEDMEN'S TOWN *of* HAMBURG, SOUTH CAROLINA

Michael S. Smith

THE History PRESS

Published by The History Press
Charleston, SC
www.historypress.com

First published 2021

Manufactured in the United States

ISBN 9781467148559

Library of Congress Control Number: 2020951859

Notice: The information in this book is true and complete to the best of our knowledge. It is offered without guarantee on the part of the author or The History Press. The author and The History Press disclaim all liability in connection with the use of this book.

Contents

Contents

Acknowledgements

This book would not have been possible without Ellen Priest and the late Scott Hunter, both former publishers of the *Aiken Standard*. It was Ellen who recruited me to lead the newspaper, and both Ellen and Scott took me under their wing. Their encouragement, guidance and support have been incalculable. I'd also like to thank Brenda Baratto, Milledge Murray and Phyllis Britt for their unique insight into Hamburg and North Augusta history. Thank you to the publishing team at The History Press for believing in me and in this previously untold story. And most of all, thank you to my wonderful wife, Nicole Pioli Smith, for encouraging me on this project.

Prologue

Thousands drive past Hamburg daily without ever realizing it, blissfully unaware they've passed one of South Carolina's most famous ghost towns, its remnants encircled by million-dollar mansions, an upscale golf course and the Savannah River. In the early nineteenth century, Hamburg embodied the nation's spirit of growth and expansionism, only to devolve into a chaotic epicenter of racial violence fifty years later.

Hamburg's history dates back nearly two centuries, when the town sprang from nothingness into a center of interstate commerce and trade. Wagons hauling cotton, wheat and other goods crammed for miles outside the town limits. Hamburg's streets were just as jammed; pedestrians had to walk blocks to safely cross the street.

The clattering of hammers and nails filled the air as workers finished laying railroad ties. Soon the first Charleston-Hamburg locomotive would roll into Hamburg, revolutionizing South Carolina transportation. In the water beyond, smoke billowed from the steamboats chugging up and down the Savannah River. Hamburg thrived.

Founded in 1821, Hamburg lured families in droves. Forty-four families moved there in the first year alone. At its peak, eighty-four buildings stood in the sprawling town. Among them were a tavern, several storehouses and an "extensive" warehouse. It was in this warehouse where 3,600 bags of cotton had been stockpiled in just six weeks, a figure that town founder Henry Shultz gleefully boasted about in newspaper editorials and legislative petitions. Shultz's voice carried weight, as he had built the first stable bridge

Historical markers off U.S. 1 immediately to the east of the Savannah River denote the location of Hamburg. *Courtesy the author.*

across the Savannah River. "Without your aid, the whole project must fail, and Hamburg [will] become what it has been, a corn field," Shultz wrote to South Carolina lawmakers.[1]

Hamburg's potential for growth and prosperity seemed limitless, much to the chagrin of Augusta, which saw its trade whittle away. Behind the scenes, however, things were far more precarious. The specter of debt saddled Shultz. Legal bills would dog him for decades until his death in 1851.

When Shultz died, his spirit died with him. Nobody carried the torch in his name, and with no heir apparent lined up to continue stumping for Hamburg, the town's decline continued unabated. This decline accelerated during the Civil War. The quartering of Confederate soldiers and fear of Union advances scared off the town's remaining first- and second-generation residents. By 1865, Hamburg was virtually deserted.

African Americans breathed new life into Hamburg during Reconstruction as freedmen flocked to the town, its infrastructure largely still in place. These pioneers, exercising their new freedom to vote, elected a mayor and town council members. Businesses reopened. Homes were reoccupied. The town even had its own Black militia. Hamburg was once again a functioning town.

This rejuvenation was short-lived, as Hamburg faced a series of existential threats that ultimately led to the town's collapse. White supremacists, jaundiced by the postwar shift of power and wealth, launched a campaign of terror, violence and intimidation to suppress African Americans statewide.

In 1876, a gang of crusty ex-Confederates and bloodthirsty vigilantes—a group euphemistically called the Sweetwater Sabre Club—targeted the African Americans inhabiting Hamburg. It was here where the white mob unleashed a torrent against the town's Black militia. Bullets zipped back and forth across Market Street, turning the town's main road into a virtual no man's land, ostensibly over a seemingly simple right-of-way dispute.

The consequences were immutable. African Americans watched helplessly as political, economic and social gains of the previous decade were wiped out within weeks. Some sympathetic white politicians condemned the slaughter, but there were no serious repercussions for the white gunslingers. Southern Democrats seized power, deferring social reform for decades. Even after the civil rights movement in the 1950s and 1960s, Hamburg's neglect persisted. The forest and swamps on which Hamburg was built reclaimed the riverside properties once more.

In recent times, discussion of Hamburg has resurfaced amid race riots and mass shootings elsewhere in the United States. Hamburg has joined

These bridge supports in the Savannah River once served as the foundation of the Hamburg–Augusta Railroad. *Courtesy the author.*

the larger debate over the appropriateness of Confederate-era monuments in today's society, including the Meriwether Monument in North Augusta.

Built to honor the one white supremacist killed during the Hamburg Massacre, a watershed event in which seven African Americans were killed, the forty-foot-tall, twenty-one-thousand-pound obelisk stands triumphantly in the heart of Calhoun Park, itself named after John C. Calhoun, a former vice president and infamous anti-abolitionist.

Today, striped green grass, neatly trimmed bushes and blooming camellias surround the statue. Sparkling blue water shoots majestically through the jets of a nearby fountain, disguising the dark message inscribed at the monument's base:

> *He exemplified the highest ideal of Anglo-Saxon civilization. By his death he assured to the children of his beloved land the supremacy of that ideal.*

In reality, the young, impetuous Thomas McKie Meriwether died moments after the opening volley, killed when a stray bullet carved a trench through his forehead as his gun overheated. Few understand this gazing at the monument.

And yet, less than three miles away, at the bottom of the hill along the North Augusta riverfront, lay the ruins of Hamburg. Only there are no monuments, lush landscaping or sparkling water fountains in Hamburg—just a forgotten town imprisoned within the forest. Ninety years of neglect have turned Hamburg into a heap of rubble, twisted vinyl and crumbling concrete. Planks of rotting wood lie lifelessly against the corner of the remaining walls. Other nearby buildings sit in similar states of decay.

Empty beer cans, torn and twisted, lie strewn across the damp, decaying leaves now blanketing the forest floor. Sunlight seldom penetrates this dense thicket as insects scurry through the bushes. It's an apocalyptic scene, hardly fitting for a town with such storied origins.

What follows is a description of how entrepreneurial spirit gave rise to this enigmatic town, as well as how white supremacy and an insatiable quest for power caused its destruction. Hamburg's origins and overarching themes predate the Declaration of Independence and continue today. It's a story extending far beyond the town's watershed event, the Hamburg Massacre, and the white supremacist monument erected to memorialize it.

It's a story of vision and ambition, a story of triumph and defeat.

It's the story of Hamburg.

Chapter 1

Before Hamburg

Settlement of the region that would later become Hamburg—and North Augusta, eventually—began centuries ago. Various American Indian tribes occupied the Central Savannah River Area, or CSRA, in one way or another prior to Hamburg's founding in 1821.[2] But it wasn't until 1670, when English settlers arrived, that the community of Savannah Town was founded.[3]

Savannah Town was located just east of Hamburg proper on land that later became known as Upper Hamburg. Today, this property lies east of where Jefferson Davis Highway, or U.S. 1, in South Carolina crosses the Savannah River into Augusta, Georgia.[4]

The English, with help from Savannah Indians, helped oust the Westo tribe that had occupied Savannah Town. Savannah Town became "a bustling place," so much so that in 1716, the English constructed Fort Moore, a military and trading outpost located nearby.[5] Trade with the Indians was so robust that it extended "all the way to the mountains and beyond."[6]

By the 1730s, the area was further settled by a group of Swiss settlers in a region called New Windsor Township.[7] New Windsor was more of a small county than an actual town, encompassing modern-day North Augusta, Beech Island and Clearwater in western Aiken County.[8]

New Windsor Township, however, struggled to find footing. The establishment of Georgia colony in 1733 and founding of Augusta, Georgia, a few years later lured settlers across the river. In addition, much of the land in New Windsor was poor and not conducive to farming.

By 1776, as the American Revolution erupted, all that remained of New Windsor Township was a smattering of small farms.[9] As fate would have it, though, a new community began to blossom.

Founded in 1770 by John Hammond, the community of Campbellton (also spelled Campbell Town or Campbelltown) quickly became ripe with commerce and trade. Hammond received a land grant of five hundred acres along the Savannah River, with which he partnered with his uncle, Le Roy Hammond, and cousin Charles Hammond to expand Campbellton.

Situated about two miles north of what would later become Hamburg, Campbellton was the region's first true competitor to Augusta. Tobacco, skins, ceramics and cotton were among the wares sold at Campbellton. By 1788, a department store had opened as well.

Perhaps foreshadowing the Hamburg-Augusta rivalry, a local trade war erupted between Campbellton and Augusta. Leading the Augusta effort was Ezekiel Harris, Hammond's fiercest rival. Harris had his own vision for cultivating the tobacco trade, and it didn't include Campbellton.

In 1794, Harris acquired 323.5 acres directly across the river from Campbellton and subdivided the land into multiple parcels. His intent was to build his own tobacco trading center, which he completed in 1797. He called it Harrisburg.[10]

To lure business away from Campbellton, Harris built a warehouse and "a good frame house" that visiting planters could use. He also advertised free ferry service to any Carolina planter provided they frequent his warehouse instead of Hammond's.[11]

As the 1790s drew to a close, the Hammond-Harris feud intensified. On the evening of May 21, 1800, at around 8:00 p.m., as Hammond was strolling through his yard, a musket blast pierced the evening air. Hammond suffered severe injuries in the attack and died one month later. Someone also torched his home.

Hammond's relatives published ads in the *Augusta Herald*, offering a $1,000 reward for information leading to the capture of his killer or killers: "We the subscribers offer the above sum for the discovery of the villain or villains or any of their accomplices, who inhumanely shot Mr. John Hammond."[12]

Nobody came forward to claim the reward, and nobody was ever charged. Some sources have suggested that Harris was involved. If so, he didn't gain anything. Financial troubles pinched Harris to the point of bankruptcy, forcing him to sell his property and move away.

After Hammond's death, Campbellton deteriorated, quickly becoming a Savannah River ghost town. The area wouldn't be developed again until the early 1800s with the arrival of a young German named Henry Shultz.

There are two popular accounts of Shultz's back story, the most popular of which holds that he fought against Napoleon Bonaparte in the Franco-

Prussian wars. Sometime in 1794 or 1795, before even reaching the age of twenty, Napoleon's forces captured Shultz but released him "upon the promise of not bearing arms any more against the French." Seldom one to cut his losses, Shultz promptly returned to the battlefield and was recaptured a few months later. A military court sentenced him to death by firing squad.[13]

Napoleon, however, showed mercy. Unable to bring himself to execute the brash nineteen-year-old, the French dictator pardoned Shultz. Rather than risk a third strike with Napoleon, Shultz immigrated to America.[14]

Another account holds that Henry Shultz was actually born Klaus Hinrich Klahn and that he sought business opportunities in Hamburg, Germany, but that the Napoleonic wars ruined him, prompting him to immigrate to America.[15]

Shultz arrived in America broke and unable to speak any English. As one account noted, "He came to Augusta…with no capital but his head and his hands."[16] He worked as a common boatman for three years, earning ten dollars per month, and he eventually made enough money to buy a tobacco flat called the *Diana*. Shultz spent the next seven years plying the river between Augusta and Savannah.[17]

At some point during his travels, Shultz realized the need for a sturdy bridge across the Savannah River. While other bridges had been attempted—two by Wade Hampton I—both had been destroyed by flood. Crossing by ferry remained the primary means of traversing the river.[18]

That changed in 1813, when Shultz partnered with twenty-nine-year-old Lewis Cooper, a native of Newark, New Jersey, and architectural genius. Cooper became the engineering brainchild behind the Augusta bridge, while Shultz served more in a financial and promotional role. Shultz would provide the timber, while Cooper performed the pile-driving and oversaw construction. Tolls would be collected to defray the bridge's cost.

Following the War of 1812, the United States entered a period of great economic prosperity. U.S. imports grew exponentially, as did exports. American cotton and tobacco were particularly popular in Europe. As demand overseas rose, so did profits. American exports hit $63 million in 1818. "The rise in export values and the monetary and credit expansion led to a boom in urban and rural real estate prices, speculation in the purchase of public lands, and rapidly growing indebtedness by farmers for projected improvements."[19]

South Carolina lawmakers, eager to increase trade opportunities, signed off on the toll bridge in December 1813, and it was completed eight months later. It cost $40,000 to build. What distinguished Shultz's bridge from previous attempts was its sturdiness. The Hamburg bridge spanned sixty feet wide and featured four-inch-thick wood floor planks. It was built for endurance. "The project was looked upon as something visionary."[20]

Another account noted that the bridge stood for half a century, "uninjured by freshets that swept away others constructed by professional architects according to the most approved scientific principles."[21] Newspapers lauded Shultz:

> *The Proprietors of the Bridge…they have campleted* [sic] *their undertaking, as to admit every kind of passage over it, with great facility and perfect safety. The piling, sleepers, braces, etc., are of the best Cypress. The whole fabric having so far been completed in a very substantial manner by Mr. Cooper, is admitted by experienced Architects, to be the most excellent piece of work of its kind ever seen in the Southern States.*[22]
>
> —Augusta (GA) Chronicle, *August 9, 1814*

> *In the present midnight of commerce, such intelligence as this is like a ray from the morning star, telling of the coming dawn.*[23]
>
> —Charleston (SC) Mercury, *1837*

Public figures showered Shultz with praise as well. In 1824, at a mechanic's festival, Colonel Joseph Hutchinson, a former Augusta city council member and two-term mayor, said that Shultz was integral to Hamburg's success. Colonel Hutchinson's words were especially noteworthy considering Shultz's ongoing feud with Augusta. "Hamburg—its rapid growth, the importance of its commerce, the industry and urbanity of its inhabitants, and the *exertions of its enemies*, call, and loudly call upon the Legislature of South Carolina to continue their judicious and liberal aid in nurturing this infant city, by nurturing the towering genius of its indefatigable and enterprising Founder," Hutchinson said.[24]

In 1835, then South Carolina governor George McDuffie issued this proclamation honoring Hamburg's founder:

> *Henry Shultz is, in my opinion, eminently distinguished for enterprise, sagacity, perseverance and public spirit, qualities of which numerous monuments, equally beneficial to the public, and honorable to himself, furnish ample testimony. Amongst these may be enumerated the Bridge across the Savannah River, so constructed as to bid defiance to the floods, an achievement often attempted before, but never successfully.*[25]

The only thing piling up more quickly than praise was crushing debt. Sadly for Shultz, unchecked spending and mounting legal bills cost him one of his greatest architectural achievements and most profitable business ventures.

Immensely wealthy at age forty-one in 1818, Shultz started planning his retirement when misfortune struck. What happened remains a matter of minor dispute, although the blame belongs in the same place. One account states that Shultz sold his interest in the bridge to John and Barna McKinne, brothers who went bankrupt following the Panic of 1819.[26] An older but more detailed version of the story states that Cooper actually sold his interest in the bridge to John McKinne in 1814, more than four years before Shultz's planned retirement. Barna McKinne didn't enter the picture until after Shultz sold his bridge interest to him in 1818, before the 1819 panic.

The McKinnes managed to repay 75 percent of a $50,000 loan, but they still defaulted. Their debts mounting, the McKinnes mortgaged their interest in the bridge to the Bank of the State of Georgia.[27] Regardless of the exact chain of events, the McKinnes bore the brunt of the blame. Shultz went ballistic. His carefully prepared retirement plans had suddenly been upended. Shultz had auctioned off all his holdings and interests, including a wharf he built, buildings, slaves and a bank he and John McKinne started. Shultz was forced to sell them all.[28]

Throwing salt on an open wound, Shultz would end up sacrificing major bridge profits. Had Shultz kept the bridge, he would've reaped more than $112,000 in toll revenue over the next eight years, equivalent to several million dollars today. Instead, that money went straight to the bank.

Shultz blamed Augusta businessmen with bank ties for the financial fiasco. His anger intensified when the bank failed and bridge ownership fell to the City of Augusta.[29] Shultz placed his own toll plaza on the South Carolina side in an attempt to recoup his losses.[30]

A protracted legal battle ensued, one that Shultz never won and basically bankrupted him. The courts ultimately issued an injunction barring him from collecting tolls on the South Carolina side. These legal fights further fueled Shultz's feud with Augusta, a feud that would persist for decades.

Chapter 2

Rise of Hamburg

Initially problematic, the Augusta bridge fiasco of 1819 wound up more of a blessing than a setback for Henry Shultz. It opened his eyes to other avenues of profit that otherwise might not have become apparent had he kept the bridge.

Upon closing the bridge, Shultz turned his attention to the coast, specifically Brunswick, Georgia, where he bought several lots in the coastal town about eighty miles south of Savannah. Shultz planned to build a canal running northwest from Brunswick to the Altamaha Valley, where the Altamaha and Turtle Rivers converged.

This first attempt to lure coastal river trade inland failed, largely due to Georgia leaders never really buying into the project. And without financial backing, Shultz abandoned the venture.[31] Brunswick wasn't a complete bust, however. It didn't take Shultz long to realize that opening direct route to the coast was profitable—just not to Brunswick. He eyed the commodity that had previously brought him success: the Savannah River.

Shultz started by imposing a toll on the South Carolina side of the Augusta bridge. If he couldn't own the bridge, he certainly would find a way to profit from it. No doubt he also derived a certain satisfaction sticking it to Augusta, which he still blamed for losing the bridge to the Bank of the State of Georgia. Lawsuits followed, though, thwarting Shultz's plan. This only intensified his hatred of the "monied aristocrats of Augusta."

Eager to settle the score, he developed his boldest plan to date. Shultz was going to build his own town along the banks of the Savannah River. He named his new town Hamburg after his hometown of Hamburg, Germany.

Hamburg would directly face Augusta, the city that had wronged him, and as payback, Shultz would steal Augusta's trade. Shultz built his town along the banks of the Savannah River overlooking Augusta. As one Edgefield historian put it, "in a fit of pique he [Shultz] vowed that he would kill Augusta's trade and build up Hamburg."[32]

At first glance, the riverside property seemed an odd location, given the region's geographical challenges. The area was wet, wooded and undeveloped. Cornfields dotted the landscape. One contemporary noted that Hamburg was built "in the midst of a hideous swamp, which he [Shultz] had ditched and drained."[33]

The area's history presented an added challenge. Hamburg was built roughly two miles downriver from the deserted town of Campbellton, creating a public perception problem. Memories of Campbellton's collapse were still fresh in many people's minds. *If Campbellton failed, then so would Hamburg*, skeptics likely thought, a notion not lost on Shultz. He arrived in Augusta in 1806, five years before Campbellton's demise in 1811. Shultz had witnessed the town's downfall firsthand.

Several things set Hamburg apart, however. For starters, the Hamburg town limits bordered the Augusta bridge, providing travelers with rapid, direct access between the two municipalities. This gave Hamburg a huge advantage over Campbellton, where the primary method of crossing the Savannah River was by ferry, both clumsy and cumbersome.

Hamburg was even more accessible by river, far more so than Augusta. Shultz also possessed a deep knowledge of the Savannah River from the years he spent plying the river. He knew the river's currents and depths more than most men, and his experiences taught him that the South Carolina side was much more favorable for navigation than by Augusta.

For about a mile, the Savannah River flowed along the Carolina side, which further aided in navigation. These currents caused river channels to be deeper, making the Carolina side much more ideal for steamboat operations, which required deeper channels. This would prove crucial because it helped establish a direct route between Hamburg and Savannah, a key port.

Hamburg had other advantages too. The town limits rose fifty to seventy feet above the river level, offering a seemingly ideal spot to build homes. The higher elevation provided picturesque views of the river while also seeming to provide some protection against floods that had historically hit the region. Nearby springs offered a fresh water source as well.

With Campbellton's downfall creating a commercial void, Hamburg came along at the right time. "As Campbellton declined in glory and wealth, and the necessity for a market on this side of the river grew, Hamburg, the offspring of the enterprise and industry of an energetic and eccentric German named Shultz, came up out of the marshes and swamps scarcely two miles below."[34]

With demand already in place, all Shultz needed was money. And the timing for that couldn't be better, either. South Carolina, like the rest of the nation, was emerging from an economic depression resulting from the Panic of 1819. Sharing Shultz's desire to compete with Augusta, South Carolina lawmakers were willing to finance anything that promised results.

As for Shultz's prior business dealings, he'd been held relatively blameless for the bridge fiasco, with the bridge's loss pinned square on the McKinnes. So when Shultz pledged that he could open a new trade route that would boost South Carolina's economy, state lawmakers assented.[35]

Shultz asked state lawmakers for a $50,000 loan to build Hamburg. His plan called for spending the first $35,000 constructing more buildings within the town and the remaining $15,000 on a new steamboat to realize Shultz's vision of a Hamburg–Charleston trade route to compete with the preexisting Augusta–Savannah route.

This is how Shultz would exact revenge on Augusta. He wanted to siphon every last dollar out of Augusta. His passion was evident in an 1821 petition to the state legislature. "Can you doubt then, that these cities are hostile, and will combine their powers to crush me if possible?" the petition read. "The secret is now divulged, that it is part of my plan to cut off the trade from Savannah as well as from Augusta. Charleston is now and will always be a better market."

In Shultz's view, denying the request was a nonstarter. The timing was crucial. Deferring action on Hamburg would lessen any chance the town would have to revive commerce. "I candidly avow, that without your aid, the whole project must fail, and that Hamburg become what it has been, a corn field," Shultz said. "If it fails now, will it ever be renewed, or ever be more popular?"

In his petition, Shultz requested a six-year property tax abatement and permission to charter a bank at Hamburg. Building a bank "will protect its inhabitants against the rivalry and oppression of these institutions in Augusta, and will supply the upper districts with the more valuable currency of our own banks."

Later, in making the case for tax breaks, Shultz threw another jab at Augusta. "The taxes in Augusta are excessively high," Shultz said. "If, as prayed for, in my memorial, all property, stock and trade, etc., in Hamburg are exempted from taxes for a few years, it will give that place an important advantage over its powerful neighbor."

With the state's help, Hamburg's business boomed. Development spread as more people flocked to the sprouting town. In an 1821 report to the South Carolina legislature, Shultz stated that 3,600 bags of cotton had been logged at the Hamburg warehouse over a six-week period, or about 600 per week.[36] After the first year, Hamburg received 17,000 bales of cotton, a figure that increased to nearly 28,000 bales by October 1823.[37]

"Before 1 July 1821," as one observer recalled, "not a house stood in Hamburg, but by 1826, two hundred houses and fifty to sixty stores served the twelve hundred inhabitants."[38]

Commerce continued to grow. By 1832, Hamburg was producing and shipping thirty-five thousand bales of cotton. The town's population stood at around two thousand.[39] "For a brief period, owing to the energies of Shultz, antebellum Hamburg rivaled Augusta."[40]

Shultz couldn't agree more. "My town has not only been built, but has wrested from Augusta that South Carolina trade of which she had possessed herself and even wins from her every day fresh portions of that of Georgia," he said.[41]

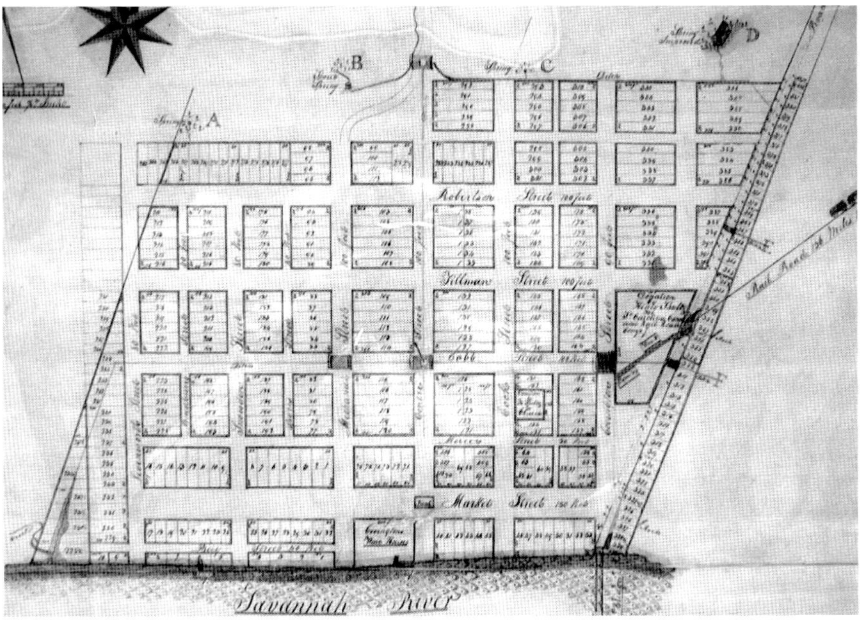

This map denotes the layout of Hamburg, as depicted by town founder Henry Shultz. *Courtesy South Carolina Department of Archives and History, Columbia.*

November and December typically were the busiest months in Hamburg. Wagons loaded with bales of cotton crept along at a snail's pace, the line often extending for miles at various ports of entry. "The road going and coming for a distance of five or six miles would be literally jammed up with wagons, rendering it almost impossible to make more than a mile an hour."[42]

One account claimed that at its peak, Hamburg received seventy thousand bales of cotton per year. The vast majority, about sixty thousand bales, arrived by wagon. And deliveries weren't limited to cotton, either. Flour, bacon and loads of other goods poured into Hamburg. "Hundreds of thousands of barrels of flour from upper South Carolina were hauled there and millions of pounds of bacon from Knoxville and all over east Tennessee came to this little Carolina trading town on wagons."[43]

Inside Hamburg, it was just as packed. Nineteenth-century historian John Chapman noted, "The streets would be so crowded with the wagons of the country people from four States that frequently people would have to walk four or five blocks before finding a place to cross."[44] Those who couldn't immediately stake out a place in line camped out in Hamburg's outskirts, waiting their turn. It wasn't uncommon to see four to five hundred tents pitched in Hamburg's periphery:

> *Many years ago, going into Hamburg with wagons loaded with cotton, we camped a short distance back on the uplands on the Edgefield side, so that we could get into market as early as possible. The sun rose clear and was shining bright and clear in the uplands, but as we drove on we found the whole valley of the river covered with a dense fog, and on that fog was clearly and distinctly defined a white solar rainbow—no colors. I saw the same, or similar phenomenon, once on the fog over the river as I walked down from Columbia to the depot to take the cars for Newberry. In both cases the bow was well defined and very distinct, without colors, having the same appearance as a lunar rainbow.*[45]

Hamburg was officially chartered as a municipality on December 19, 1827, and rechartered in 1830. Fittingly, Shultz became its first mayor.[46]

The burgeoning town even had its own publication. Not long after the town's founding, the *Hamburg Gazette* became the town's first newspaper, hitting the streets in February 1823. Frederick W. Pleasants was the publisher. The *Gazette* published weekly on Wednesdays. Few editions exist today. The earliest known edition was published on July 23, 1823. Consisting of four pages, the *Gazette* contained a hodgepodge of national news, local news and

THE HAMBURG GAZETTE.

Vol. 1. Published by Frederick W. Pleasants, Hamburg, (S. C.) Wednesday, July 23, 1823. No. 23.

ALLEN DERMOT

A Tale of the Revolution.

LETTERS

DOCTOR FORD.

THOMAS MORRIS, Esq.

JOB-PRINTING,

In all its various branches executed neatly, accurately and with dispatch at this office.

The July 23, 1823 edition of the *Hamburg Gazette*, Hamburg's first newspaper.

poetry. The *Gazette* routinely published various commodity prices, offering a unique glimpse into Hamburg's commercial activity.

In 1823, according to the *Gazette*, flour fetched between $8.00 and $9.50 per barrel. A bushel of corn cost $0.60 to $0.70, while a gallon of whiskey, described as "good" and "scarce," sold for $0.40 to $0.50. Steel, tobacco, rice, rum, cognac and molasses were also among the plethora of goods traded at Hamburg.[47]

Shultz's steamboats often made local news. The *Gazette* reported that one of Shultz's vessels, aptly named the *Hamburg*, completed the journey from Charleston to Hamburg in five days with "full freight," arriving on July 18, 1823, and departing three days later. Another vessel, the *Commerce*, which arrived on July 22 and also carried full freight, was said to have transported a green turtle that weighed a whopping 390 pounds.[48]

In the years that followed, other newspapers published on and off in Hamburg, although not all of them were complimentary. Shultz was particularly disdainful of the *Carolina Galaxy and Commercial Gazette*, although the impetus of this feud isn't entirely clear. On October 4, 1834, in its inaugural edition, the *Galaxy* published a story that quoted Shultz speaking derisively of the newspaper:

> *Having noticed in several papers, a prospectus for a paper to be published in the town of Hamburg, and feeling it my duty to inform the public, that the intended Editor is an entire stranger to myself and to this community, and the publication of the intended paper does not meet the approbation of myself and many of the citizens of Hamburg, with a few exceptions only, and recently several subscribers have withdrawn their names; it will, therefore, not be considered a paper of this place, and has no connexion* [sic] *with the town whatever.*[49]

The *Galaxy* didn't exactly turn the other cheek. In a rebuttal, an unsigned editorial response said only two readers had canceled their subscriptions, not the "several" Shultz had asserted. Readers were invited to view the *Galaxy*'s subscription list at its offices. "We have the unqualified and tangible approbation and patronage of almost every citizen of Hamburg; and numerous subscribers elsewhere," the newspaper wrote. Then the newspaper threw a few barbs Shultz's way:

> *If we could conceive that the public or ourself* [sic] *cared one sixpence about the originator of this controversy, we should perhaps notice this*

> *impotent attempt to shackle the liberty of this press, and the arrogant and unwarrantable interference with our private concerns, at some greater length. But the game is not worth the candle.*[50]

Despite these occasional skirmishes with the press, Shultz's reputation as an entrepreneur remained intact. In 1814, he and Lewis Cooper opened the first stable bridge across the Savannah River, opening new opportunities for trade and commerce between Georgia and South Carolina. "From the first this bridge paid good dividends on the investment."[51]

In 1817, Shultz "again astonished the natives" by building a wharf that was fully operational.[52] It was built along two riverside tracts of land that he leased from the City of Augusta for $60,000. While natives remained astonished, Shultz wasn't. He knew something most people didn't: the Savannah River was fertile ground for development.

Also in 1817, Shultz became a partner in the first fully functional steamboat operation. It wasn't long after that the South Carolina legislature granted Shultz exclusive rights to operate steamboats on rivers in the state. Shultz soon had a small fleet of steamboats, each traveling from Charleston to Hamburg.

The first vessel was named the *Commerce* and was followed by the *Hamburg*. Newspaper stories boasted that despite traveling upriver, the boats were capable of reaching Hamburg in five days. In subsequent years, five other vessels launched—the *Edgefield*, the *Pendleton*, the *Augusta*, the *Henry Shultz* and the *Maid of Orleans*. All featured direct navigation between Charleston and Hamburg.[53] "Thus in thirteen years the poor immigrant had become one of the outstanding business men of Augusta."[54]

Shultz's thirst for revenge ultimately led him to found Hamburg. In 1821, Shultz spotted an undeveloped stretch of swampland and cornfields that he thought would be the perfect place to build a new town. The location wasn't far from Campbellton, itself a riverside trading post that seriously competed with Augusta before fading away.

On June 6, 1821, Shultz signed a lease for 330 acres, agreeing to pay $500 per year for six years to start building his new town. "He was to drain the swamp, lay off lots and streets, build warehouses and storehouses, erect wharves, and lease lots to others."[55]

Hamburg boasted breathtaking riverside views. Four natural springs located nearby offered abundant fresh water. Shultz had selected an ideal site on which to build:

> *It* [Hamburg] *reported to the South Carolina legislature in the fall of 1823 that it contained 176 houses, 1 Church, 1 Bank, 1 Post-Office, 1 School, 39 Stores, 4 Public Houses, 2 Warehouses, 114 Private Dwellings, 1 Printing-Office, 1 Market-House, 2 Physician's Offices, 1 Druggist's Store, 1 Silver-Smith, 2 Blacksmiths, 1 Butcher's House, 1 Tailor's, 1 Saddler's, and 1 Painter's.*[56]

Within a year, close to one thousand people lived in the steadily growing town. Shultz's obsession of stealing Augusta's trade was coming to fruition. "My town has not only been built, but was wrested from Augusta that South Carolina trade of which she has possessed herself and even wins from her every day fresh portions that of Georgia," Shultz said.[57]

Chapter 3

Hamburg and the Railroad

Shultz's steamboat monopoly prospered. Vessels were regularly docking and departing Hamburg's wharves, each packed with passengers and cargo. For every ship that docked, Shultz reveled in knowing that was one less ship that would stop in Augusta. "This taking Augusta will repent to the end of time, for I shall be able with permission of the Great Ruler to teach that once great city a lesson ever to be remembered how to tamper with common sense and the hard earnings of an honest man."[58]

But as Shultz gloated over his own ingenuity, the face of interstate transportation was about to fundamentally change. In 1827, Charleston was growing increasingly concerned that Savannah River levels had fallen unusually low that year. One of Hamburg's primary advantages was its proximity to deep navigation channels. Dropping river levels threatened to take this advantage away.

Hamburg and Charleston also started trading more with Savannah instead of each other, further cutting into each other's bottom line, although Charleston was hit the most. In 1827, the Holy City's cotton bale intake plummeted to 9,450 bales, while Savannah took in nearly 43,000 bales. Charleston merchants knew that they needed a faster, better way to Hamburg, so they turned to the state for help.

Initially, the city's leaders considered building a canal, although that was quickly abandoned since finding enough water to fill it was deemed unfeasible. With river navigation options drying up, Charleston looked into chartering a railroad to Hamburg.[59] It didn't take long for the railroad to gain traction.

In March 1828, the South Carolina legislature commissioned a feasibility study into operating a Charleston–Hamburg railroad. Abram Blanding, the state's superintendent of public works, was tapped to conduct it. Blanding's findings validated the hopes of Charlestonians. "I can unhesitatingly pronounce, that such a road is perfectly practicable," Blanding said. "I think I am warranted in going farther, and saying, that no line of road of the same extent, connecting two such important points as Charleston and Augusta, can be found in the United States, where the same facilities of graduation and construction are combined in the same degree as on this."[60]

Blanding knew that building a railroad would present unique engineering challenges. Whereas Charleston was close to sea level, the nearly 140-mile track reached a peak of about 545 feet near present-day Aiken, about seventeen miles east of Hamburg.

The good news was that from Charleston to Aiken, the incline was gradual, extending 123 miles, or about 4.5 feet per mile. "On the Charleston side of the summit, the ground is remarkably regular, and I am clearly of the opinion that with very moderate expense, a graduation may be obtained, on which the approach to Charleston will no where have a rise of more than 10 feet to the mile," Blanding noted.

It was the final seventeen miles that posed problems. From Aiken to Hamburg, the elevation dropped considerably. In Blanding's four-page report, he estimated the decline at 391 feet, or about 23 feet per mile. That made the proposed line far too steep for trains of the day to traverse. "On the other side of the summit, all the difficulties are to be found in the way of the locomotive engine, as a power on this road," Blanding said. "At first view, these difficulties appeared formidable indeed."

Blanding considered several options, two of them utilizing horses. One proposal called for using horses for the final seventeen miles. Another suggested using horses for a nine-mile stretch near Hamburg and locomotives for the remainder. "On these nine miles, an additional number of horses may be used," Blanding said. "Although between the summit and Charleston, locomotive engines alone should be used; all the carriages might be brought up from Hamburgh [*sic*] to the summit by horses and then be conveyed to Charleston by steam power."

The simplest and most expedient plan involved operating a locomotive engine directly from Charleston to Hamburg. But first engineers needed to tackle the elevation issue. Not only was the terrain hilly, it was also irregular. A series of valleys and ridges rippled through the landscape, hardly suitable terrain for locomotives of the time. Trains heading down steeper stretches of the summit would struggle to brake, especially in wet or icy conditions, increasing risk of derailment. And trains departing from Hamburg couldn't muster the momentum to reach the summit without assistance.

A more winding route was considered. Just as a beginner ski trail coils its way down the mountain, a more circuitous rail line with gentler grades would mitigate the danger associated with traversing steep hills. But this option required more track, driving up costs.[61] As one 1894 trade publication put it:

> *To have overcome this difference in elevation in grades or curves, over and around which the primitive locomotive could have passed drawing a train, would have involved the sacrifice of immense distance not warranted by the then existing conditions or demands. The incline was developed as the best and most economical way of making the descent into the valley.*[62]

Blanding estimated that building an all-locomotive line capable of navigating the rugged landscape would require six extra miles of track. Engineers solved the dilemma with an innovative solution: the inclined plane. It was the inclined plane, with its steam-powered pulleys, that allowed heavy locomotives to traverse the steep slopes between Aiken and Hamburg. "The remainder of the ascent must then be gained by a stationary engine working on an inclined plane, of any angle of rise which may be deemed advisable," Blanding said.[63]

Development of the inclined plane was absolutely crucial in extending the railroad to Hamburg. It was also responsible for "connecting much of the upland of South Carolina and Georgia commercial traffic to Charleston."[64]

The inclined plane's premise was relatively simple, with the configuration resembling a modern-day roller coaster. A pair of parallel tracks ran from the top of a hill to the base. At the summit, a hoisting rope wound around a wheel and extended the length of the plane. This rope connected to one car at the summit and another at the base, each balancing the other out.

Each set of cars was connected to "brake cars," which utilized lever brakes to keep the train from charging out of control in the event of cable failure. Every twenty feet, a series of horizontal wheels called rollers supported and guided the two-and-a-half- to three-inch rope.[65]

The final piece to the inclined plane was a stationary steam engine, which powered the rope. Two train cars—one at the bottom and the other at the summit—were raised and lowered simultaneously until both reached more level ground. Once that happened, the locomotives would continue under their own power. The inclined plane represented an advancement

Builders of the Charleston and Hamburg Railroad used the inclined plane to help navigate dramatic elevation changes between Aiken and Hamburg. *Courtesy Library of Congress, Prints and Photographs Division, Washington, D.C.*

over two preexisting modes of transportation: steamboats and horse-drawn buggies.

There were three inclined planes along the final seventeen miles of the railroad. One was located in Aiken, near what's now Park Avenue and Laurens Street.[66] The plane was routed south of property that later became Aiken Golf Club, which opened in 1912, and through what's now Hitchcock Woods, one of the nation's largest urban forests.[67]

In 2017, inside Hitchcock Woods, archaeologists excavated parts of the railroad believed to be from the original inclined plane.[68] The railroad remnants were located in a region known as the Sand River, so named because it's essentially a river of white sand subject to significant storm water runoff during major rainstorms. It was this runoff that eroded enough sand to reveal the railroad planks. Archaeologists theorize that erosion displaced the planks from their original location over the years.[69]

A 2018 study found additional artifacts in the sand and also along the predicted route of the original South Carolina Railroad. The study determined that these artifacts did originate from the inclined plane, calling their discovery "profound" and their survival "remarkable."

The discovery was so significant the study noted that no original wooden rail track exists anywhere in the United States, nor does any intact iron-capped wooden rail exist anywhere in the world. "These tracks deserve recognition as one of the most important artifacts of early American industry, and possibly as one of the most important artifacts of the early history of the U.S. in existence today," the study concluded.[70]

The "Best Friend," the first locomotive built for rail service in the United States. *Courtesy Library of Congress, Prints and Photographs Division, Washington, D.C.*

Trains were immensely superior to other modes of transportation in antebellum South Carolina. They could carry much more freight than by horseback. Trains were much faster than steamboats, capable of completing the journey in hours instead of days. And they opened new possibilities for passenger travel. In 1835, a steam engine typically completed the 136-mile journey from Charleston to Hamburg in twelve hours, leaving the port city at 6:00 a.m. and arriving at 6:00 p.m.

Railroad travel didn't break the bank, either. A one-way ticket from Charleston to Hamburg cost $6.75. Children under twelve years old and "colored persons" (reflective of the antebellum mindset) could ride for half price. A baggage limit of seventy-five pounds was set.[71]

Fares increased to eight dollars the following year, owing largely to the railroad's popularity and technological advances. Travel times plunged by three hours or more for a one-way trip from Charleston to Hamburg, with trains capable of traveling twenty-five miles per hour.

By 1836, trains leaving at 7:00 a.m. arrived around 4:00 p.m. The return trip was even quicker, with trains departing Hamburg at 6:00 a.m. and reaching Charleston by 2:15 p.m. South Carolina Canal & Rail Road Company advertisements promoted breakfast and dinner for passengers, while promising to stop no more than five minutes to restock for wood and water.

Over time, the railroad industry realized that inclined planes were becoming cumbersome. Bottlenecks often occurred as train cars bunched up, waiting their turn to traverse the inclined plane. Sometimes the backups were so great that passengers and crew were forced to spend the night in Aiken before completing the final leg to Hamburg. "The labor and time required for this method of transfer cannot be fully appreciated by one who witnessed the operation."[72]

Still, the inclined planes remained in operation until 1852, when a new innovation negated the need to lift and lower rail cards by pulley. Dug by slave labor, the "Aiken Cut" punched through several chunks of previously impenetrable terrain.

By cutting through rugged terrain instead of routing around it, train tracks could be laid with far shallower grades. This seven-mile swatch ran from downtown Aiken to Warrenville, an Aiken County hamlet about seven miles west-southwest of Aiken.[73] Trains continued using the line until 1964.[74]

While inclined plane logjams were an issue, they were integral in the founding of Aiken—ironic, considering that a motivation for building the railroad was so Charleston could tap into the cotton market in Hamburg. Rather than wait for inclined plane logjams to clear, many travelers opted to spend the night in Aiken, creating a need for accommodations, shops and other conveniences.

Aiken flourished. On July 4, 1835, an Independence Day celebration there drew between eight hundred and one thousand people. Trains by then were already running three times a day at 9:30 a.m., noon and 2:00 p.m. Later that year, the growing township of Aiken officially incorporated, forming on December 19, 1835.[75]

An 1839 petition to the state legislature following a disastrous fire noted that Aiken held appeal due to "desirability of the climate…for invalids at all seasons of the year" and also as "a place of retirement for our fellow citizens of Charleston and other places."[76]

Today, Aiken boasts a permanent population of 29,524 people and has become a prominent equestrian community. It's also only about seventeen miles from the Savannah River Site, one of the nation's largest nuclear storage facilities and research hubs and an important employer. None of it, though, would've happened had it not been for the inclined plane.

Ironically, Hamburg never fully embraced the railroad. While Aiken flourished because of passing trains, not one Hamburg resident bought stock in the proposed line after the State of South Carolina chartered it. Charleston investors gobbled up the railroad stock.[77] Besides, the initially tedious nature of train travel at the time was well known. Boredom remained an issue through at least 1849:

> *The rail-way journey from Orangeburg to Augusta was extremely monotonous in scenery and incident. The scenery by the way-side alternated between cozy swamps embellished with cypresses, cultivated fields, and extensive forests of oak and pine, garnished occasionally by a tall broad-*

> *leaves magnolia. The country was perfectly level through Barnwell District, until we passed Aiken into Edgefield.*[78]

Another reason railroads never gained steam in Hamburg was because they competed with the town's steamboat and wagon trade. In 1845, when the Greenville and Columbia Railroad contemplated making Hamburg a terminus for one of its lines, Hamburg balked. Greenville and Columbia even offered to pony up $50,000 to finance the line, but Hamburg still resisted. The town's unwillingness to embrace growth and change proved costly. "In those days there was great prejudice against railroads, and the citizens of Hamburg were afraid that it would take away their wagon trade, so the road was built to Greenville, and fully one-half of Hamburg's trade was taken away."[79]

In related matters, partly owing to the railroad rush and also perhaps anticipating a loss of business in Hamburg resulting from the Greenville and Columbia Railroad's aborted plans, the South Carolina Railroad pushed forward with plans to extend its line into Augusta, Georgia.

Henry Shultz himself was lukewarm on railroads. Always more of a river man, Shultz once said, "[E]xperience has shown that though passengers may prefer railroads, merchandise prefers the rivers."[80] In 1839, after opting not to seek election to Hamburg's town council, Shultz turned his attention back

Sketch of the Savannah River from the Augusta side by B.J. Lossing, with Hamburg visible across the river. *From B.J. Lossing's* Pictorial Fieldbook of the Revolution, *vol. 2 (Harper Brothers, New York, 1852).*

toward transportation, his eyes set on building "a Turnpike from Hamburg to the mountains."

Humility hardly one of his strengths, Shultz in an op-ed reminded the *Augusta Chronicle & Sentinel* that he "had won a victory in eighteen years of war" since founding Hamburg in 1821. As for the turnpike, the idea was an extension of a pledge he made to open trade routes between Hamburg and his native Hamburg, Germany, and other European nations. He even hinted at supplying labor from his homeland. "Intending to visit Europe next spring, I might bring a number of my countrymen as laborers to serve in that enterprise," Shultz said.[81]

Hamburg profited initially from the railroad despite the town's indifference to it. During the week of June 20, 1835, the railroad carried 655 passengers and more than seven hundred bales of cotton to Charleston. Receipts totaled about $3,561.94, exclusive of a mail contract, or about $102,000 in 2018 dollars.

One train was even named after Shultz, curious given his reluctance to embrace railroads. The *H. Shultz*, built in 1835 by Rothwell, remained in service for nine years before it was retired in 1844.[82]

In the 1830s and 1840s, whether Hamburg liked it or not, it's clear that the railroad industry had a major impact on the town's economy. It was the terminus of a 136-mile line, the longest in the world at the time, increasing the town's publicity. Railroad development was responsible for "connecting much of the upland South Carolina and Georgia commercial traffic to Charleston."[83]

Inevitably, Hamburg's growth attracted criminals and con men. Perhaps the most notable were the infamous con men claiming to have captured a live "gyascutus," a mythical animal resembling a fox-wolf hybrid with legs much shorter on one side than the other. This enabled the beast to circle hillsides at fantastic speeds, but only in one direction.[84]

More of a lumberjack folk tale than fact, the gyascutus was allegedly discovered in the 1840s in the northwestern United States. This "monster" with "fierceness and dangerous qualities" quickly became a hit at fairs and carnivals, often fetching hundreds of dollars from eager townspeople hoping to catch a glimpse of the elusive gyascutus. Just as the curtain to the stage rose, the monstrous beast managed to break free. "Gentlemen and ladies, the Gyascutus has broke loose!" one of the hosts exclaimed. As frightened ticketholders fled for their lives, the showmen conveniently escaped, only to reappear in another town, gyascutus supposedly in tow.[85]

This happened in Hamburg sometime in the late 1840s. Apparently, it took four horses to haul the raging beast across the river from their stables in Augusta to Hamburg. As the hour of the show approached, throngs of curious Hamburg residents and visitors jammed the streets, although only a few dozen lucky people scored tickets to the show hall. Tickets cost one dollar apiece. Inside the hall, a curtain "depicted a likeness of the most uncouth creature ever seen, or that any imagination ever conceived."

Just as the beast was about to be unveiled, "a large growl was heard behind the curtain." Roars, shrieks and hisses followed, "more terrifying than any the lions and tigers and all the beasts of the jungle ever made." Then came the fateful words: "The Gyascutus is broke loose! The Gyascutus is broke loose!"

Ticketholders fled in a panic. "Some never stopped running until they were safe in Augusta. Some thought they could clear the Savannah [River] at a leap, tried it, and landed safe in the mud on the Carolina side."

Curiously, as in other cities, the showmen disappeared, never to be seen in Hamburg again. Even more curiously, the horses that allegedly hauled the gyascutus to Hamburg were spotted the next day "and were very quietly standing in their stalls in Augusta and eating their oats."[86]

Leading up to the Civil War, Hamburg still did strong business. In 1859, a reporter for *DeBow's Review* described Hamburg as "the best interior cotton market in the South, or, at least, is held so by all South Carolinians." The reporter's adulation of Hamburg's commercial appeal was described in this fashion:

> *One cause of this is perhaps the close competition with Augusta, another the plucky character of the people…but doubtless the main reason is the cheapness of freight and the facilities of transportation to the seaboard by means of the Savannah River, the South Carolina and the Augusta and Savannah Railroads. The merchants are willing to work for small profits. There are some daring cotton speculators in the town, many of whom have realized large fortunes while others have lost. Probably there is no other town of equal size in America where more or larger commercial vicissitudes and successes occur.*[87]

Well into the 1880s, trade was still taking place in Hamburg, thanks largely to the expansion of rail lines in Aiken County. The addition of a rail line linking Edgefield and Trenton to Aiken allowed farmers to ferry wagonloads of cotton bales to Hamburg and Augusta, where they could sell their crops and buy supplies.[88]

Chapter 4

Hamburg in Decline

Henry Shultz envisioned building a new town and possessed the ability to articulate that vision to men of influence. This quickly propelled Shultz to prominence. For all his construction, however, Shultz never could build financial security for himself.

At a time when many were cashing in on locomotive fever, the German entrepreneur was reneging on loans. He'd long burned through the $50,000 the state loaned him to build the town, spending most of the money on legal bills in a failed bid to reclaim the bridge he lost to Georgia bankers. His relentless pursuit of revenge against Augusta left him virtually penniless.

Destitute and desperate, Shultz attempted suicide by sticking a loaded gun into his mouth. The weapon, however, was pointed upward, so instead of killing him, the bullet exited through his forehead and left "indelible marks of powder" on his face. Oddly enough, he fully recovered from the attempt on his life.[89]

Shultz wouldn't recover from his financial predicament so easily. He never escaped from the shadow of insolvency, his downfall seeming to foreshadow the downfall of Hamburg itself. Through thick and thin, though, Shultz never stopped advocating for his beloved town. "The State must have failed to fulfill some of its promises, for after Shultz was ruined he was often seen in Columbia during the sessions of the Legislature with his long overcoat dangling around his heels and the mark of Cain upon his brow."[90]

Some of Shultz's legal woes crossed into the criminal courts. On July 30, 1827, two women entered the town of Hamburg saying that they had been robbed. They told a bystander that an African American youth had stolen a trunk and fled into some bushes. It didn't take long for the authorities to capture the youth, who quickly confessed to the theft. The youth said he stole the trunk at the request of a white male by the name of Joseph Martin. Both the boy and Martin were traveling to Hamburg when they encountered the women, the youth said.

Martin denied any involvement, and a warrant was sworn against him and the boy. The boy was whipped for his role in the alleged heist. Martin suffered an even greater punishment. On the following morning, perhaps acting out of a twisted sense of chivalry for the two defenseless women, Shultz sought out Martin in an attempt to retrieve the trunk. Two other men—Alexander Boyd and David Lynar—joined Shultz to dispense justice.

Reason quickly gave way to rage as Shultz began whipping and beating Martin, who fell into a ditch. Martin wound up swallowing a large amount of mud and water and later died. Now Shultz was facing criminal charges.

Shultz immediately felt remorse over the attack. The *Augusta Chronicle and Advertiser* reported that Shultz brought the wounded Martin back to his home and sought medical attention. The newspaper report suggests that Martin wasn't seriously injured from the attack itself but rather succumbed to his wounds after suffering from an acute case of bilious fever, likely brought on by oppressive summer heat. Shultz, Lynar and Boyd were charged.[91]

Lynar absconded. He eventually died before the trial. Shultz and Boyd were taken into custody and jailed in Edgefield until the trial. They were found guilty of manslaughter and sentenced to six months in prison. The defendants were also ordered to be branded with the letter *M* on their thumbs, but both later received gubernatorial pardons.

Shultz wept over the man's death, his contrition eliciting sympathy from many in Hamburg.[92] "They were deeply overcome, and many turned aside to hide the tears that they could not repress. Many of the most respectable and wealthy citizens stepped forward and begged…that he might be untied, and offered themselves as guards on the way to Jail, but the request was not granted."[93]

Not long after his release, Shultz found himself jailed once again, this time for insolvency. He was released only after assigning all of his property to his debtors.

Shultz's legal battles continued for decades. In February 1850, in a packed courtroom, the U.S. Supreme Court finally heard arguments in Shultz's ongoing bridge lawsuit against the Bank of the State of Georgia. As in the past, things didn't go his way. "There were few matters of fact immediately before the court of a nature to sustain rhetorical episodes, but such as presented themselves were touched with consummate art."[94]

Curiously, among those arguing on Shultz's behalf was Andrew Pickens Butler, a U.S. senator. Butler is perhaps best known as lead author of the Kansas-Nebraska Act of 1854.[95] He was also an uncle of Matthew Calbraith Butler, a Confederate general who would later play a major role in the Hamburg Massacre and its aftermath.[96]

Andrew Pickens Butler, former U.S. senator and uncle of Confederate general Matthew Calbraith "M.C." Butler. *Courtesy Library of Congress, Prints and Photographs Division, Washington, D.C.*

Shultz never succeeded in his quest to reclaim the Augusta bridge. He died virtually penniless in 1851. He was buried on Shultz's Hill, less than a mile east, looking down on the Savannah River. According to local legend, Shultz was buried standing up and facing Augusta so he could always keep an eye on his river-town rival.

Hamburg's feud with Augusta didn't die with Henry Shultz. In the years following Shultz's death, the two towns clashed over bridge tolls, a common practice in Hamburg's history. Initially, tolls served an economic purpose, mainly by Augusta in an attempt to lure back trade it had lost to Hamburg. Through the early 1840s, cotton flowed freely into Hamburg. Wagons packed the roads on land, and steamboats shipped large quantities of cotton via the Savannah River. Hamburg had become "a great cotton mart, besides supplying its full quota of groceries to the up-country, and correspondingly lessening the trade of Augusta."

Over time, tolls evolved into a political weapon wielded by both cities. One of the more colorful clashes occurred in 1852, in the months following Shultz's death. In 1850, Shultz had secured a charter with the State of South Carolina to toll the South Carolina side of the Augusta bridge at Hamburg. After his death in October 1851, Augusta believed that the charter died with him.

Then along came General James Jones and Joseph J. Kennedy, assignees and administrators of Shultz's estate. In January 1852, the men re-invoked the 1850 charter and proceeded to erect a toll gate. Hamburg leaders endorsed the plan.

Augusta grew alarmed. In the city's view, it owned the bridge and held proprietary rights over tolling. In response to the Hamburg toll, Augusta adopted a resolution to institute its own toll on the Augusta side, its amount matching the Hamburg toll. The toll dispute continued to intensify. At one point, Augusta reportedly threatened to fire a cannon at the gate. Shultz's heirs responded in kind:

> *Jones replied that two could play at that game, reminding him that Shultz had left a couple of old cannon* [sic] *on the hill in Hamburg, which was six hundred feet above Augusta, and that he would certainly return the fire.*

In the end, despite the bravado and chest thumping, the bridge dispute reached an amicable resolution. Both sides agreed to dismantle their toll gates.[97] Additionally, Augustans with stake in the bridge agreed to pay Shultz's heirs $10,000 in accordance with his will.[98] "As soon as reliable information shall be received by his Honor the Mayor, that said attempt to collect such contribution, improperly called Toll, is abandoned, the rates of toll at said Bridge, shall thenceforth be the same as they are at present," the resolution read.

Eager to recapture its lost cotton trade, Augusta eventually waived tolls on wagon traffic heading into Georgia. Wagons bound for South Carolina still had to pay.[99]

Augusta also went after Hamburg's river trade. For decades, Hamburg's steamboat operation had siphoned business from Augusta. Favorable currents flowing on the South Carolina side made Hamburg a much better place to do business. Augusta needed a new strategy if it was to reclaim the river trade. The answer was as innovative as it was damaging to Hamburg.

The Augusta Canal's origins date back to 1845, when the Augusta City Council appointed Henry Cumming to carve the new waterway west of the Savannah River. Its aim was to allow river traffic to bypass the Savannah River. The canal would also be devoid of the tricky currents common in the river, making the canal a safer, quicker option.[100] "Navigation by pole boats on the upper Savannah [was] both difficult and dangerous over the shoals below the locks at the head of the canal."[101]

The canal would run for nine miles, branching off from the Savannah River about five miles north of Augusta and rejoining the river just south of town. It was funded by $100,000 in bank loans backed by the City of Augusta. A 4 percent property tax would be levied, and in exchange, property owners would receive stock in proportion to the taxes they paid. An observer at one planning meeting noted that in similar projects elsewhere in the United States, property values skyrocketed 500 percent.

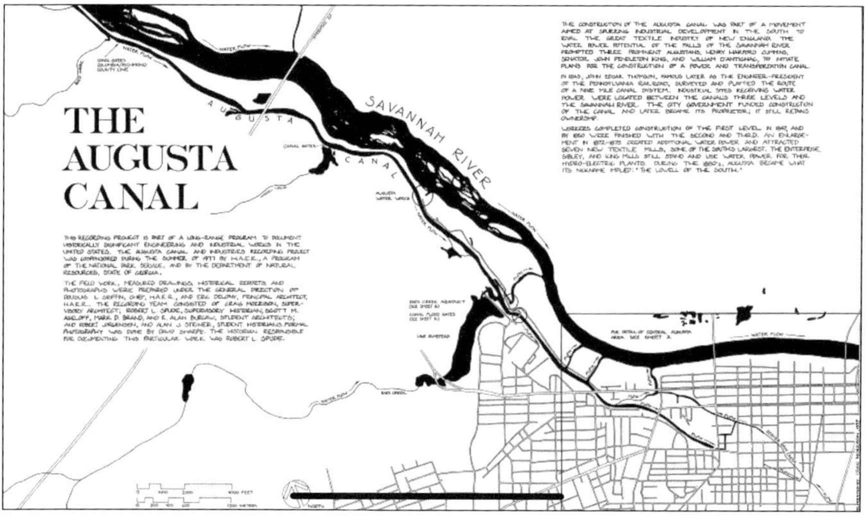

This image depicts the Augusta Canal in relation to the city of Augusta and the Savannah River. *Courtesy Library of Congress, Prints and Photographs Division, Washington, D.C.*

The observer further estimated that properties along the canal route stood to increase by 10 percent before the first shovels turned earth. While these projections may have been exaggerated, it's clear that property owners stood to gain financially.

"The unanimity with which this meeting decided on the adoption of the measures proposed [only one voice being heard in the opposition], leaves little doubt of the ultimate completion of this great work," one observer said. "The sum necessary to complete it is so insignificant in comparison with the utility that it promises."[102]

Interestingly, Hamburg and the surrounding region brushed aside any notions that the canal would hurt business. In fact, initial news reports suggest the community actually embraced the canal. A November 1847 news report published two years after the venture began suggested the canal would be beneficial to Hamburg and the Upstate region: "We congratulate our planting friends near the River, on the favorable prospect, and hope that such measure will be taken in the upper Districts as may lead to an appropriation for the River, not only to the head of the Canal but to the junction of the Tugalo and Seneca."[103]

Other media wrote that the canal would divert trade away from Hamburg. "Hamburg does not promise to fulfill the hope or follow up the energy and dispatch which presided at her birth," the *Charleston Daily News* wrote in August

1849. "The Augusta Canal has already drawn off a considerable portion of her cotton trade, and the Columbia Railroads to Greenville and Charlotte will in a few years, perhaps, place her among the enterprises that *were* but *are* not."

The *Hamburg Republican* actually defended the canal, shrugging off any notion that it would seriously erode Hamburg trade. An editorial noted that Hamburg remained a robust commercial hub, receiving 65,000 to 70,000 bales of cotton, 1,200 to 1,500 barrels of flour and 175,000 to 200,000 pounds of bacon per year:

> *As for the Augusta Canal it has taken from us perhaps some ten thousand bales of cotton, but that is only temporary. Hamburg, though not based on a rock, stands like Hamburg of the old world, where her water advantages will always protect her from petty Canals or Railroads on the Mountains.*[104]

But cotton losses weren't temporary, as the newspaper had asserted. Trading continued to decline into the 1850s. Hamburgians took notice, including the town's founder. Despite his financial difficulties, Henry Shultz's voice still carried weight. So when he sounded the alarm against the Augusta Canal, peopled listened.

In a December 1845 letter to the *Coosa River Journal*, Shultz noted that the canal caused potential "obstructions" that could impede navigation of the Savannah River and asked the South Carolina legislature to order the state superintendent to investigate. If the superintendent found any obstructions, then he should "take all proper steps to have them removed, and that all the facts of the case be submitted to the next Legislature," Shultz said.[105]

The canal debate persisted, and as it did, a new transportation craze exploded onto the scene. As one anonymous letter writer put it, the region needed to embrace plank roads lest Hamburg "dwindle down to completely nothing."[106]

Plank roads were lumber-based passageways that promised a smooth ride for horses and carriages. The writer proposed building a plank road to overcome the sandy soils between Hamburg and Edgefield:

> *This would obviate the deep sand, and vastly improve the condition of the Martin Town Road. Whatever is done should be done quickly. A delay of twelve months will be too late.*

Two months later, the Hamburg & Edgefield Plank Road Company officially incorporated. In December 1849, petitions to begin building plank roads were swiftly submitted to the General Assembly. One petition requested funding to make the Savannah River more navigable between Hamburg and the mouth of the Augusta Canal, although that petition never stayed afloat.

A second petition calling for the creation of a company to build a twenty-six-mile plank road from Hamburg to Edgefield found more favor. The petition received a favorable report, and at about the same time, the Hamburg & Edgefield Plank Road Company officially incorporated.[107]

Today, popular local folklore in North Augusta implies that plank roads were around long before the 1840s and 1850s, associating the wooden passageways with Hamburg's golden age. The truth, however, is that plank roads were built in a desperate attempt to reinvigorate Hamburg's trade, not enhance it.

To this day, the City of North Augusta website incorrectly credits Henry Shultz with building the plank road, an assertion that can't be true because when Shultz died in 1851, the plank road wasn't even completed. Additional legs weren't ready for travel until 1853, two years after his death.[108] By 1850, Shultz was also penniless; there was no way he could have afforded to finance a twenty-six-mile plank road.

It is true that Shultz stated intentions to build a turnpike road from Hamburg to the North Carolina mountains. Philosophically speaking, he likely would have supported building the plank road as a means of combating Augusta's efforts to steal Hamburg trade. However, there's no concrete evidence that Shultz saw his plan to fruition.

Shultz wasn't among the principals of the Hamburg & Edgefield Plank Road Company, either. The company's leadership consisted of H.A. Kenrick, president; Charles Hammond; and Josiah Bland. Simeon Christie. S. Trowbridge was the superintendent.[109]

Plank roads weren't limited to Hamburg or Edgefield. The plank road rage spread throughout South Carolina, including Graniteville near Aiken, where entrepreneur William Gregg sought his own plank road charter.[110] Plank roads quickly became the rage in South Carolina. In 1853, a *Cheraw Chronicle* editorial insisted that the wooden roads were superior in every way imaginable:

> *If a wagon and team could be found which would last carrying a load 4000 miles, over an ordinary road, the same wagon and team could carry the same load 8000 miles over a plank road, and then be in good condition. But it is useless to tell men so who are penny wise and pound foolish.*[111]

Plank roads emerged as a transportation fad in the 1850s. *Courtesy Library of Congress, Prints and Photographs Division, Washington, D.C.*

Construction promptly commenced on the Hamburg and Edgefield plank road, which had a $50,000 budget. Ads seeking workers ("Negro" workers mainly) quickly popped up in local newspapers.[112]

In October 1851, the first leg of the Hamburg and Edgefield Plank Road opened. It extended about eight miles from Hamburg, stopping at Cherokee Ponds and Sweet Water.

Tolls started at one cent per mile for individual horseback travelers. One-horse carriages cost two cents per mile, while two-horse carriages and two-horse wagons paid three cents. Wagon rates increased incrementally for each extra horse, maxing at five cents per mile for four-, five- and six- horse wagons. Failing to pay the toll carried a twenty-dollar fine.[113]

By January 1853, the Hamburg and Edgefield plank road was substantially completed, with twenty of twenty-six miles open for travel.[114] Plank roads, however, proved to be more fad than functional. They were clunky and unkempt, and their neglect was a constant source of irritation for wagon travelers. In an 1856 op-ed, one such person was especially perturbed by the tolls travelers had to pay: "Plank Roads, we fear, will prove comparative humbugs....About ten miles of the Edgefield and Hamburg Road are rougher than any portion of dirt road we are acquainted with."[115]

Little changed two years later. The *Edgefield Advertiser* blasted the plank road operators as inattentive and incompetent, accusing them of "violating both duty and law" by collecting tolls and not reinvesting the money in upkeep. The editorial especially took issue with the plank road company's cavalier attitude that suggested travelers with grievances could choose to use dirt roads instead. "The thing [the road] has grown worse and worse, until now its abominable condition is too censurable to merit either patience or forbearance. It has become a vexation almost intolerable. It is the subject of every traveler's abuse....There are not three miles smooth in the twenty-six."[116]

By 1860, the vast majority of plank road companies had gone bankrupt.[117]

Chapter 5

HAMBURG, CIVIL WAR AND RECONSTRUCTION

Many historical accounts depict Hamburg as having disintegrated into nothingness by the time the Civil War erupted. One of these accounts, on which much of Hamburg's history is derived, originates from John Chapman's *History of Edgefield County*, published in 1897. "Some time in the year 1862, or 1863, I rode through it with a friend in a buggy, and it was then the most lonely, desolate place I had ever seen," Chapman noted. "What it is now I know not. I have never seen it since, except from the windows of the rail road coach as I passed down the road."[118]

While Chapman provided invaluable insight into how people lived in Hamburg, this account is not entirely accurate. In actuality, commerce continued into the 1860s. Cotton sales carried on. Pharmacists sold medicine. Weapons dealers peddled guns. And grocers sold food. Hamburg's golden age may have passed, but it was far from a ghost town.[119]

Hamburg served an important military function during the Civil War as well. The town was a gathering place for companies called into service, its location along the South Carolina Railroad between Atlanta and Columbia giving it strategic importance. The town itself became pressed into service to accommodate Confederate soldiers.

Hamburg was also one of many South Carolina locations targeted by tax collectors to collect revenues in support of the Confederacy. "Tax Payers will make out an inventory of everything they possess on the 17th day of February 1864, that was valuable, and bring it with them, or send it by their Agent," a typical notice read.[120]

In August 1861, a Hamburg women's group gave the Edgefield Rangers, a company of South Carolina's Sixth regiment, a massive sendoff that included a presentation of a bugle. Leading the sendoff was Lucie S. McKie (Hammond), daughter of company commander Captain Andrew J. Hammond and a Hamburg resident.[121] A local newspaper marveled at the fiery rhetoric from her address to the Rangers:

> *Now, whenever you appear upon the field of conflict, let your beautiful flag be ever waving over you, the sound of this bugle ever falling on your ears, reminding you more forcibly of the cause in which you are engaged. We feel assured that you, the Edgefield Rangers, will either return victorious, or else, every man of you, meet a glorious death.*[122]

Hamburg was also home to one of the Civil War's most famous regional soldiers. Born on February 9, 1843, Berry Benson and his brother, Blackwood, joined the Hamburg Minute Men while they were still teenagers—seventeen and fifteen, respectively. In January 1861, nineteen days after South Carolina seceded from the Union, the Benson brothers were mustered into service and promptly departed for Charleston. "We left in a storm of cheers, Father giving us a little money, a little good advice, and his blessing," Berry Benson said.[123]

The elder Benson served as a marksman during the war, although his main claim to fame is that he escaped twice from Union prisons. In one instance, he dug a tunnel to escape from an enemy prison in Elmira, New York. His ingenuity earned him a furlough, so Benson embarked for Hamburg. "Everybody was rejoiced to see me at home, and I enjoyed the change for a few days, but it was only a few days."

Soon news reached Hamburg that Union general William T. Sherman was swiftly marching through Georgia. Nobody knew where Sherman was heading, and some feared that he might pass through Hamburg. Benson departed for the coast on January 17, 1865.

Benson would continue fighting until the Civil War officially ended, although he and his brother never surrendered. They proudly returned to Hamburg and then moved on to Augusta, their rifles at their side.[124]

In the war's later years, Hamburg gradually shed its commercial heritage, becoming a de facto military outpost instead. By November 1864, Hamburg was maintaining a "very warlike appearance," according to one newspaper, which noted that Hamburg merchants endured great hardship as soldiers quartered in the town conscripted it for their own use. That often meant

A statue of former Confederate soldier Berry Benson stands atop a seventy-foot spire in downtown Augusta. *Courtesy the author.*

militarization of private businesses. "Nearly every available building has been pressed for the use of these troops, which has caused much inconvenience to the merchants and citizens of the place," the article stated.

In one instance, a merchant whose business was pressed had to relocate goods from his store to the parlor of his residence. "This is very tough, but necessity is the mother of invention, and knows no law, and all we can do in these war times is to grin and bear it."[125]

An alarming report appeared in the *Edgefield Advertiser* one week later. Governor Milledge Bonham, in an address published in December 1864, announced plans to organize various militias into companies and ordered them to rendezvous at Hamburg. The announcement came in response to the Battle of Atlanta in July 1864 and its aftermath, when General Sherman began his infamous "March to the Sea," a three-hundred-mile campaign from Atlanta to Savannah along which Sherman employed scorched-earth tactics, leveling infrastructure or private property in his wake.

On January 7, 1865, when Benson was likely resting in Hamburg, a member of the Aiken Mounted Infantry from Barnwell District proudly wrote that in response to South Carolina governor Luke Bonham's call, the infantry assembled in Hamburg in preparation for Sherman's possible arrival. When Sherman swung south, so did the infantry. "They promptly responded to the call, and as the enemy advances toward Savannah, they were well employed in guarding the ferries and crossing places on the river, having gone within twelve miles of Savannah."[126]

Sherman's morale-busting strategy invoked fear among Confederates and is credited with helping to end the war. What made Sherman's advance so fearsome was that nobody knew where his forces were headed, including Bonham, who feared that Sherman's forces planned to head due east toward Augusta and, eventually, to Columbia, so he ordered Confederate companies to Hamburg.

It's easy to see why Bonham thought that Sherman was heading for Augusta. From Bonham's perspective, Augusta was a tempting target. Situated about seventy miles west of Columbia, it offered easy access by land to Columbia and by water to Savannah and Charleston. Controlling Augusta meant cutting off critical Confederate travel routes.[127]

Sherman had other ideas though. As Confederate troops amassed at Hamburg, Sherman's forces turned southeast, although some forces pushed east toward Augusta as part of Sherman's ruse. In time, however, Sherman's army rendezvoused in Milledgeville, his true destination. From there, Sherman's army faced little resistance en route to the Savannah River, reaching the Savannah city limits right before Christmas. The Confederate army surrendered four months later.[128]

Union general William T. Sherman. *Courtesy Library of Congress, Prints and Photographs Division, Washington, D.C.*

After Sherman's march, Hamburg and Augusta saw an influx of Savannah refugees. They reported that while Sherman was ruthless when it came to destroying property and infrastructure, the Union general treated civilians with kindness.

Unfortunately for African Americans, they didn't receive the same sort of respite that their white overseers reported. Savannah refugees reported that Sherman wasn't a great liberator, as some slaves had believed. Sherman cared neither for emancipation nor equal rights. "Sherman has taken no slaves from their masters. Those who wish to leave do so. Those who wish to remain do so," the *Edgefield Advertiser* stated.[129]

This account aligns with others concerning the Union general, accounts that depict him not as a great emancipator but rather just as racist as his contemporaries in the South, his disdain for disunion the only thing outweighing his disdain for African Americans. Historian Robert K. Murray characterized Sherman in this fashion:

> *Few Northerners were basically more sympathetic to the pre-war Southern way-of-life or closer to that area's inhabitants in thought than this dreaded Attila of the West. Only on the question of disunion and secession did he openly demur from the opinions of his Southern hosts. With slavery apparently he had no quarrel whatsoever.*[130]

Hamburg's decline rapidly accelerated after the war. Although the village was largely spared from military attack, fires and floods caused considerably more damage than artillery and shelling ever could. Sadly, Hamburg's needs took a backseat to the state.

South Carolina's top priority after the war was to rebuild the state's railroad system. Rail lines had taken a beating during the war, and getting them back on track was a top priority, with the Columbia & Hamburg Railroad sitting near the top of the list. "It will prove an artery of trade of invaluable account to the widest scope of country, as well as the immediate section of the South through which it passes," the *Edgefield Advertiser* wrote.[131]

So desperate was South Carolina to maintain the railroad that the state was willing to contract with African American laborers, even during the war. Newspapers often published classified ads seeking paid Black laborers to work on the Columbia & Hamburg Railroad. One such ad sought twenty laborers in Leesville, South Carolina, about fifty miles to the east. "Liberal wages will be paid and especial care taken of the Negroes. Negroes employed to work on the Railroad will be exempted from labor on the Coast fortifications."[132]

In the meantime, Hamburg suffered a series of natural disasters, the latest in a series to come. In November 1864, a large fire destroyed a warehouse near the Savannah River, taking with it 1,200 to 1,500 bales of cotton. Authorities suspected arson.[133]

Arson was also suspected in rash of fires targeting another warehouse owned by Major Charles Hammond. The first fire erupted in December 1864, claiming 50 bales of cotton. A few weeks later, a massive inferno consumed Hammond's warehouse, destroying another 1,400 bales of cotton, causing $1 million in damage. "The fire was one of the most sudden that has occurred here lately, before the citizens were aware of it, the entire building was enveloped in the devouring element."[134]

One month later, a large frame building the government operated as a hospital on Mercer and Covington Streets burned to the ground, taking with it the home of a Hamburg resident. A second home belonging to Hamburg resident William Hill was damaged as well, a loss considered tragic since his downtown shop had recently been pressed by the Confederate army for its own use, rendering him essentially homeless.[135]

A massive flood added to the misery. The flood of January 1865 completely covered the town and much of Augusta. "It was completely and wholly submerged, there not being a dry spot within the corporate limits." In Hamburg, a mother and two children tragically died in the freshet. While water levels didn't rise quite as high as previous floods, the river current was much stronger, splashing through city streets at a brisk twelve miles per hour.

Another account of the flood stated that "hundreds of poor families" suffered greatly, losing furniture and belongings. The South Carolina Railroad Bridge across the river survived, but railroad tracks through Hamburg were mangled and shredded like matchsticks. Embankments collapsed as well. "Hamburg yesterday presented the spectacle of a complete wreck. But one house—the corner brick opposite Hammond & Lock's cotton shed—escaped the invasion of the watery foe. Fences and buildings were all gone, and an especial spite seems to have been manifested towards the temples of Cloacina, which we saw scattered about in odorous profusion."[136]

Outside of town, plantations suffered greatly. "Most of the plantations are overflown, and hundreds and thousands of cattle, hogs and other stock have been washed off and drowned."

If there was one saving grace, it's that the Confederate troops in town as well as railroad workers were integral in saving the South Carolina Railroad Bridge from raging floodwaters.[137] But for ordinary citizens, the January 1865 flood was the last straw. It generated an exodus from Hamburg to Augusta, foreshadowing what was to come over the next fifty years. "Several families have moved in the past few days from Hamburg, having become so thoroughly disgusted with the late flood, that they now seek comfort on this side of the water."[138]

The departure of residents, in turn, took a toll on local businesses. In the years following the war, Hamburg merchants tried their best to resume a normal life. Some took to the newspapers to advertise that they were still open. One such ad by William Hill, a kitchenware merchant from Hamburg, proudly proclaimed his wares:

> *I take this method of announcing to you that I am still at my old stand, where I am conducting the same old line of business, which comprises the usual assortment of shelf and heavy hardware & cutlery. Also Tin Ware, which I manufacture in all its Styles and Patterns.*[139]

Sadly for Mr. Hill and others, they just couldn't hold on as the departure of Hamburg businesses to Augusta continued during Reconstruction, no doubt following their former patrons across the Savannah River.

In April 1866, Levy & Asher, a clothing and jewelry store that did business in Hamburg, left town and reopened on Augusta's Broad Street. A newspaper advertisement announcing the move characterized Hamburg in a peculiar way: "Having lived many years in Hamburg, the former principal market of Western South Carolina, we have selected the above Goods with a view of meeting the wants of our old customers."

William Hill, the Hamburg kitchenware merchant, eventually threw in the towel as well, leaving Hamburg for Augusta in 1869. "Our old friend Wm. Hill has left Hamburg. We hope his Edgefield patrons will follow him."[140]

As they did, it stripped any hope of Hamburg regaining its past status as a trading hub. Even wealthy residents, including Jeremiah Stokes, the president of the Hamburg Bank who owned a posh riverfront home, weren't immune to financial losses. The banker reported personal losses of $150,000, roughly $2.3 million in 2019 dollars.[141]

The misery continued into the late 1860s, when another destructive fire claimed one of Hamburg's last remaining major structures. In 1868, on a bitterly cold Christmas Day, flames consumed the Hamburg Hotel. The fire soon spread to several other buildings. It was so cold that firefighters reported that water froze almost immediately after coming into contact with the frigid air.[142] "Reconstruction, with its hells and horrors, crushed out the last lingering hopes in the hearts of the property holders."[143]

Chapter 6

Eve of a Massacre

On what should've been a festive anniversary of the signing of the Declaration of Independence in Hamburg, tumult and turmoil marked the days preceding the nation's centennial, culminating in a clash between two white men and the town's African American militia and setting up one of the deadliest race riots in American history.

Things started going awry about thirty minutes into an Independence Day celebration that featured a series of drills by the town's militia, when a pair of hooligans named Thomas Butler and Henry Getzen approached. Accounts vary on whether Butler and Getzen intended to interrupt the parade or the militiamen taunted the two men, but the outcome was crystal clear. The father of Thomas Butler swore out a warrant against the militia's captain, ostensibly for unlawfully blocking a public road.

Prince Rivers, the town's magistrate and also African American, presided over the initial court hearing on July 6, 1876. But the hearing soon turned into bedlam, and the hearing was postponed to July 8. In rescheduling, Rivers hoped that cooler heads would prevail.

About an hour before the hearing, Rivers was still at his home in Hamburg when he heard a knock. Rivers opened the door to find Dock Adams, Allen Attaway and a few other members of the Hamburg militia standing outside.

Adams captained the militia that was at the center of brewing hostilities. Attaway was its second lieutenant and an Aiken County commissioner with a penchant for outspokenness. Both Adams and Attaway knew that tensions had not cooled, as Rivers had hoped. During the day, armed

Union colonel Thomas W. Higginson, commanding officer and ardent supporter of Prince Rivers. *Courtesy Library of Congress, Prints and Photographs Division, Washington, D.C.*

whites had been descending into Hamburg. A peaceful resolution seemed increasingly unlikely. Adams knew this, which is why he sought Rivers a few hours before the hearing.

"Judge Rivers, I can't appear before your court today, for I feel that you are unable, and your court is unable, to protect my life," Adams said. "I believe my life to be unsafe."[144]

Rivers weighed Adams's words with his usual pensiveness. An escaped slave from Beaufort County, the forty-two-year-old Rivers had led a structured, disciplined life. Large and broad-shouldered, Rivers served three years in the Union army under Colonel Thomas W. Higginson before settling in Hamburg. Higginson called Rivers a man "of distinguished appearance," praising his ability to command and to command respect. "As to actual discipline, it is doing no injustice to the line-officers of the regiment to say that none of them received from the men more implicit obedience than Color-Sergeant Rivers," Higginson said.[145]

But for all his accolades, Rivers could not stop the waves of white supremacists gathering in Hamburg on July 8, 1876. By the 1870s, bands of white vigilantes calling themselves "rifle clubs" had proliferated in the Palmetto State. One such club, the Sweetwater Sabre Club, organized a few miles north of Hamburg and recruited many notable members, including Ben Tillman, who later went on to become a U.S. senator. At the age of twenty-eight, Tillman made clear the rifle club's mission:

> *It had been the settled purpose of the leading white men of Edgefield to seize the first opportunity that the negroes might offer them to provoke a riot and teach the negroes a lesson as it was generally believed that nothing but bloodshed and a good deal of it could so well to answer the purpose of redeeming the state from negro and carpet bag rule.*[146]

With more and more white gunmen filtering into town—some of them drunk—even Rivers knew that Adams was correct—that cooler heads would not prevail. "Well you must use your own judgment, of course, if your life is unsafe," Rivers said. "If these men intended to take your life of course I can't protect you. I haven't protection enough to protect you. My constable can't do much."

"That is my belief, and for that reason I don't want to go before your court without you [forcing] me to," Adams answered. "If I am killed you will be responsible."[147]

Hamburg hadn't always been this hostile, and Rivers hadn't always been this deferential. But by this point, Rivers knew that he was basically a lame duck justice, that his days holding public office were numbered.

White vigilantes assembling in town had plans for their own brand of justice. Rivers was powerless to prevent it; the best he could hope for was to find a way to find some sort of compromise that would prevent bloodshed. The grim state of affairs stood in stark contrast to the joyous celebration Rivers had participated in thirteen years earlier.

The date was January 1, 1863. A twenty-nine-year-old Prince Rivers stood proudly on a makeshift stage in Port Royal, South Carolina, not far from the Beaufort plantation where he had been enslaved less than a year earlier. Clasping an American flag in his left hand, Rivers grinned as a crowd of more than three thousand people below danced and feasted on oxen barbecue, all celebrating their newly gained freedom.

Hours earlier, President Abraham Lincoln had issued the Emancipation Proclamation, declaring freedom for all slaves in Confederate states. For Rivers, the victory was far more personal. In a matter of months, he went from slave to decorated soldier. Higginson held Rivers in such high regard that the Union colonel entrusted Rivers with overseeing prisoners and daily policing of the camp, noting his talent for tracking down deserters. "There is not a white officer in this regiment who has more administrative ability, or more absolute authority over the men; they do not love him, but his mere presence has controlling power over them," Higginson said. "He writes well enough to prepare for me a daily report of his duties in the camp; if

"Sgt. Prince Rivers [standing between American flags] receives the colors of the First South Carolina Volunteers, Port Royal, South Carolina, January 1, 1863." *Courtesy House Divide: The Civil War Research Engine at Dickinson College, http://hd.housedivided.dickinson.edu/node/32578.*

his education reached a higher point, I see no reason why he should not command the Army of the Potomac."

One time, while at a parade in New York, a racist mob assaulted him at the sight of chevrons on his sleeves. Rivers held off the mob until police arrived. "His features are tolerably regular, and full of command, and his figure superior to that of any of our white officers, being six feet high, perfectly proportioned, and of apparently inexhaustible strength and activity," Higginson continued. "His gait is like a panther's; I never saw such a tread. No anti-slavery novel has described a man of such marked ability. He makes Toussaint perfectly intelligible; and if there should ever be a black monarchy in South Carolina, he will be its king."[148]

After the Civil War, Rivers threw his hat into the political arena. In 1867, Rivers became a registrar in Edgefield. One year later, he was elected to the South Carolina House of Representatives, joining the first Black majority legislature elected in this state. Also in 1868, Rivers was chosen as a delegate to the South Carolina Constitutional Convention.

Prince Rivers (*fourth row from top, far left*) of Hamburg was among many African Americans to serve in the South Carolina House of Representatives during Reconstruction. *Courtesy Library of Congress, Prints and Photographs Division, Washington, D.C.*

Back in Hamburg, he was appointed town magistrate, an appointment he held for twelve years, despite repeated attempts by white supremacists to remove him from the bench.

Rivers is credited as being a founder of Aiken County and was also instrumental in forming Hamburg's all-Black militia in 1870, later serving as its major general. In 1871, he was elected intendant in the Hamburg Town Council elections. African Americans won a majority of seats in a Republican sweep.

White Democrats, however, worked to erase African American gains through intimidation and violence. They denigrated the transformed town, scowling at the concept of Black leadership. Democratic newspapers were more than happy to gin up their white supremacist readership:

> *The town of Hamburg. Alas! Troy nods to her fall. Indeed, it may almost be written.…Its few houses, mostly in a dilapidated condition, and occupied mainly by idle, thieving negroes, the pools of standing water in and around it, with almost as entire absence of all trade and animation, contrast sadly with the promise of its early days.*[149]
>
> —Southern Enterprise, *Greenville, South Carolina*

> *Poor old God-forsaken Hamburg—once the flourishing cotton mart of Western Carolina—now the abode of a greater number of the most consummate Radical thieves, plunderers, and "curs of low degree," in proportion to population, than ever cursed any other spot on the broad face of this green earth of ours. The few decent people yet residents of that luckless town (and there are a few) have our warmest commiseration....A freshet forty feet high is now the only hope for the redemption of Hamburgh* [sic]. *Brethren, let us pray.*[150]
>
> —Edgefield (SC) Advertiser

Also elected in 1871 were Allen Attaway (Adams's second lieutenant) and Louis Schiller, an ostracized county treasurer and a newspaperman of Jewish descent.[151] A former Confederate soldier, after the war, Schiller switched from the Democrat to Republican Party. To white Democrats, this was almost as offensive as African Americans holding office. Democrats later accused Schiller of supplying Adams's militia with munitions, generating consternation among other whites.

As if election results weren't upsetting enough to ex-Confederates, an old squabble with Augusta over tolls reared its ugly head once again. A few days after the Hamburg election, Augusta enacted an ordinance that required foot passengers crossing the Savannah River from Hamburg to Augusta to pay a toll. This escalated tensions, as the toll was clearly designed to block African Americans from entering Augusta. "A large proportion of the foot passengers across the river are impecunious colored vagabonds from Hamburg, and, as may be imagined," one newspaper stated. "It made the hot blood of chivalrous Africans boil with indignation to think that when they wished to reach the gin-mills of Augusta they would either have to swim the raging Savannah [River], or else pay over to a rebel city government the nickels won by honest industry at draw-poker or the string game."

Hamburg retaliated by ordering that any cow spotted wandering across the river be impounded, a surprisingly common occurrence at the time. In order to retrieve their wayward cattle, owners had to fork over five dollars per impounded animal. "Many, many Ku Klux cows have been in the habit of daily wending their way across the Savannah, and have found no pasture so sweet or so tempting as that afforded by the verdant marshes of Hamburg."[152]

This, too, gave newspapers fodder for ginning up the Democratic base. Some news reports spoke of a "prospective war" between Hamburg and

Augusta. Most newspapers blamed Rivers, claiming that he personally posted a sign on the Hamburg side of the river, spelling out the new policy:

> *Affairs seem rapidly approaching a crisis, and we had better begin to prepare for war. P.G. can furnish a navy, and the other wards an army, which we think will be more than sufficient to crush the haughty Rivers in the event that he proclaims hostilities. If war does come, we will never stop until the Hamburg government is overthrown, and our victorious forces have entered the enemy's capital in triumph, and then we will annex the little burg and keep it straight.*[153]

As the bridge controversy raged, the white-run media also started targeting John Williams, a Hamburg resident serving as sergeant-at-arms of the South Carolina legislature. He also was a colonel of the colored militia that Rivers helped form the previous year.

In early March 1871, before the municipal election, Williams tried to cross the bridge from Hamburg to Augusta. He was either unable or unwilling to pay the ten-cent toll and promised the gatekeeper that he would pay when he returned. The gatekeeper agreed and let Williams pass. However, a few hours later, when Williams tried to cross back into Hamburg, he pretended that he had already paid, according to a news report. "Fortunately, about this time the deputy made his appearance on the scene, and Williams was exposed in his attempt to defraud the city and made to shell out the necessary nickels before he was allowed to proceed."[154]

The press, again eager to appease its Democratic base, reported without evidence that Williams threatened to torch the bridge if Augusta didn't rescind the toll. "Other colored belligerent Hamburghers declare that they seriously intend to set up a toll gate on their side of the bridge," the report said.[155]

Williams flatly denied the report. In an op-ed, he wrote that he was several miles away when the alleged dustup occurred. Williams didn't specify his exact whereabouts but adamantly denied threatening to torch the bridge:

> *I wish, through your valuable columns, to pronounce the above statement false in every particular. It is the evident desire of some parties, to me unknown, to raise a feeling against me in Hamburg, where I reside, but, unfortunately for them, my reputation as a peaceable citizen will refute any such false statements.*[156]

Eventually, the bridge toll fuss faded, although it was far from the last racially charged clash in and around Hamburg, and Dock Adams knew it. He was well aware that armed whites were pouring into town. He knew that declining to appear in court was only postponing the inevitable.

Ever since the hearing on July 6, white threats against Adams and his militia had been on the rise. On the day after the hearing, while in his home next to the militia's drill room, Adams heard a group of white men plotting outside. Among them was Reverend J.P. Mealing, a local preacher, whose words were anything but Christian. "That's where that damned company drills. Tomorrow they are going to have a trial, and we intend to kill the captain of that company before he gets away from that court," Mealing allegedly said, according to testimony Adams provided a few months later.

On July 8, the day of the rescheduled trial, Adams spotted Henry Getzen; Tommy Butler; Butler's brother, Harrison; and their father, Robert J. Butler. All were armed with sixteen-shooters. At least another seven pistols lay in their buggy.

Soon the number of armed men grew to thirty, and within thirty minutes, about one hundred men had gathered in front of George Damm's grocery store. Everyone was armed, and many were loading up on liquor while boasting about how "they were going kill every God damned nigger in Hamburg that day and especially Dock Adams."

That's what prompted Adams to seek out Prince Rivers.[157]

Chapter 7

Ned Tennant Riots

Thomas Butler and Henry Getzen couldn't believe their eyes when their buggy rolled into Hamburg.

On a hot, humid Fourth of July, in celebration of the nation's centennial, an all-Black militia captained by Dock Adams was drilling in the middle of Centre Street, the main road through town. To the two brothers-in-law, it was the most audacious thing they'd ever seen. African Americans drilling in the middle of the road they always traveled, the road leading home to the Butler plantation. Butler and Getzen halted their buggy about two blocks from the parade, staring ahead with incredulity.

The Butlers took a proprietary view of Centre Street, viewing it as an extension of their estate. Their property bordered Hamburg, and Centre Street literally fed into the plantation. Tommy Butler himself called it "my father's street." In actuality, "his father's street" was nothing more than a wilderness of weeds, a pair of ruts cutting through the overgrowth. It was along these ruts that the Butlers often traveled.[158]

Gazing at the drilling militia, Butler and Getzen murmured in revulsion. There were many reasons for their consternation—the sight of armed Black men marching in a street that white men thought belonged to them was chief among them.

It had only been a day since Butler, while riding on the very same street, clashed with a different group of Black men. As Tommy later described, a man named Dave Phillips cursed and threatened him. Phillips belonged to the town's all-Black militia.

In Butler's version of the story, he was hurrying home when three Black men halted his carriage in the street. He claimed that Phillips cursed at him from a nearby porch. Instead of ignoring the insult and continuing home, Butler stopped and turned to Phillips, wanting to know what prompted the cursing. At that moment, two armed men walked up from a nearby house. Outnumbered, Butler left, he claimed. "They cursed me for a damn son of a bitch, and said that they would shoot me," Butler said.[159]

Of course, Tommy wasn't exactly a paragon of virtue. Two years earlier, he and an African American man named Samuel Spencer, a successful cotton factor in Hamburg, were involved in an unspecified altercation.[160]

Years later, while in his late thirties, Butler found himself facing an attempted murder charge. In 1893, in front of one of his favorite watering holes in Hamburg, the bombastic Butler was involved in a shootout with a white hotel owner and his family. Butler was later acquitted.[161]

Getzen, too, harbored deep resentment toward African Americans and Hamburg in general, a resentment that he inherited from Reverend J.P. Mealing, the uncle who raised him.[162] Getzen had a violent reputation; he was known for beating African Americans and one time had shot at such a group for no real reason.[163]

The Butlers dreaded traveling through Hamburg. Like most whites, they regarded it as a dangerous slum, where crime and corruption ran rampant. Thieves often targeted trains hauling cotton through Hamburg, something the media blamed on overtly strict town ordinances requiring trains to slow to a snail's pace when traveling through town.[164]

White Democrats especially despised Jim Cook, the town sheriff. Stories swirled about the perverse pleasure Cook took in arresting travelers, usually on trumped-up charges of drinking from Ben Spring, a water well situated in the middle of Market Street. Offenders were fined five dollars plus another one dollar for the arrest. "I never seen the men drinking out of the spring, but I saw that money paid," John Lee, a Hamburg resident, once mused.[165]

In contrast, the Butler Plantation was vast. Dwarfing Hamburg, it spanned about 5,600 acres, or nearly nine square miles. Cotton and corn fields blanketed the landscape. Overlooking it all was the two-story, five-bay antebellum Butler home. Built in 1859, the "Star of Edgefield" boasted panoramic views of the surrounding countryside. A dirt walkway lined with crepe myrtle trees led to the front porch. It was from this stately perch that the Butlers looked down on Hamburg—literally and figuratively.[166]

The "Star of Edgefield" in modern-day North Augusta was the former home of Robert J. Butler. *Courtesy the author.*

Raw racism certainly factored into their loathing. But the proliferation of African American militias had greatly elevated racial tensions over the past two years, with the first occurring in Ridge Spring in August 1874:

> *A disturbance between the whites and blacks at Ridge Springs* [sic], *Edgefield County, on the line of the Columbia & Augusta Railroad, last week, at one time threatened serious trouble. The arming and mustering of the negro militia and some threats made by them, caused much apprehension among the whites, and led to their sending to Augusta for arms and men. A quantity of arms and a company of men were speedily sent, with a promise of more, and soon several hundred armed men were on the ground. The blacks have given up their arms and the trouble seems to be at an end.*[167]

Not long after the Ridge Spring fracas, another clash involving a Black militia occurred just north of Edgefield. Known for his flamboyant dress and demeanor, a man named Ned Tennant captained an all-Black militia in Edgefield, earning him the reputation of being a "notorious militia captain." One newspaper dubbed him the "Great Black Hawk of the Savannah."[168]

In September 1874, Tennant claimed that unknown assailants shot into his home, which was located on the plantation of M.O. Glover, a few miles north of Edgefield. Believing that white supremacists were responsible, Tennant mustered his militia.

Naturally, newspapers portrayed Tennant as the antagonist. The *Edgefield Advertiser*, without providing evidence, described him as a "notoriously mischievous fellow." The *Newberry Herald* noted that Tennant's insurrection exhibited a "warlike attitude" and that he "made threats of a violent and incendiary nature." Tennant threatened to burn his landlord's property and "clean out the country," according to another account.[169]

In response, many whites organized their own paramilitary forces to counter Tennant's troops. Commanding one such group was Matthew "M.C." Calbraith Butler, a former Confederate general descended from a long line of powerful South Carolina politicians. Paramilitary "rifle clubs" and ordinary citizens took up arms as well. The combined forces totaled about four hundred, matching or exceeding Tennant's militia.[170] "Additional reinforcements flocked to each side, and for several days a collision seemed inevitable."

South Carolina was quickly losing the peace. Franklin Moses, the state's Republican governor, gave both sides three days to disarm and disband. His proclamation fell on deaf ears, prompting Moses to frantically ask President Ulysses S. Grant to send more federal troops to ensure order. Grant brushed off the request, responding that he thought troops already stationed near Edgefield were sufficient.[171]

Order was finally restored when Tennant agreed to surrender his arms to federal troops. Tennant also signed a written agreement to "not to tap a drum or assemble the negroes at any time in the future without informing some responsible white men."[172]

Newspapers credited whites—General Butler, in particular—with helping to quell hostilities. Butler cosigned a proclamation issuing a stern warning to Tennant and his followers. In part it read:

> *Prior to the organization and arming of the militia the most perfect tranquility and good order prevailed in our community. The placing of arms and ammunition in the hands of ignorant negroes in a time of profound peace and tranquility…is entirely without justification…the leaders of these misguided people, who are responsible for their violence and lawlessness, must not misconstrue this forbearance into a temporizing with their recklessness.*[173]

The "truce" didn't last long. In January 1875, someone torched General Butler's home, with the blame placed squarely on Tennant. There was no direct evidence implicating Tennant, but bad blood quickly gave rise to the Second Ned Tennant Riot.

Parties consisting of deputies and rifle club members went looking for Tennant, but he wasn't home. One group searching some nearby woods stumbled on a detachment of his militia, which opened fire. Nobody was hurt in the opening salvo, although matters quickly escalated. Tennant assembled a militia to combat the roughly one thousand whites who were now searching for him.

Tennant quickly fled to Columbia, citing safety concerns. Back in Edgefield, he faced charges of attempted murder and assault with a deadly weapon with intent to kill General Butler and others. He eventually surrendered to a Columbia judge, who guaranteed his safety.

That judge was Thomas J. Mackey, a Republican who at the behest of newly elected governor Daniel Chamberlain embarked for Edgefield to investigate the Ned Tennant riots.[174] Once there, Mackey jailed Tennant but later released him on a $1,000 bond. Tennant filed his own criminal complaint against General Butler and ten other men, charging them with assault and battery with intent to kill.

Serving warrrants to the former Confederate general and his acolytes proved easier said than done. For various reasons, the Edgefield County sheriff feared both sides. It took a full day to secure a deputy willing to arrest General Butler and his men. "The Sheriff of the County appears to be a worthy and inoffensive man; but his whole intelligence and sense of duty seem to have lapsed into a strong instinct of self preservation," Mackey later said. "He was afraid to enter the Merriwether [*sic*] Township, because the black people didn't know him, and the white people did know him."

Butler and the other ten men surrendered peaceably. They admitted that a conflict occurred but denied many of the particulars. The eleven men were each granted $1,000 bonds and released.

In his initial report to his good friend Chamberlain, Mackey concluded that restoring peace and tranquility in Edgefield required immediate action. Mackey recommended that Tennant's militia surrender its arms to the state and also for the rifle clubs to disband, which Chamberlain did via executive order:

> *It is impracticable for me at present to present a full exhibit of the facts in regard to the condition of Edgefield County, which facts are of the gravest*

> *concern to the State.... Suffice it now to say that, in my deliberate judgment, no such iniquity as the County government of Edgefield has been inflicted upon any portion of the English-speaking race since the Saxon wore the iron collar of the Norman.*[175]

None of the participants of the Second Ned Tennant Riot appear to have faced any real consequences. In November 1875, Tennant succumbed to tuberculosis, while Butler remained very active targeting Black militias, including the Hamburg militia eighteen months later.[176]

Tensions over Black militias continued through 1875. In August, at least eighty African Americans were rounded up in four Georgia counties near Augusta. A telegram whose origin was never authenticated called on African Americans to shoot and kill as many white people as possible. The telegraph read, in part:

> *You tell brother Jack to kill every white man and get every gun he can. Make out to the white men that you are sorry that they think we will hurt them, and if you know of any man that has got money make them give it to your treasurer, and we need it. Have all your companies ready. Kill with axes, hoes, pitchforks, and get gun powder and shot as you kill.*

Newspapers identified the insurrection's leader as General Joseph Morris, a former slave supposedly radicalized by the spoils of newfound freedom. Colonel Robert Morrison, a resident of Burke County, Georgia, and Morris's former master, said that Morris was never a commissioned officer, although he presented himself as one.[177] Morris and others also allegedly implicated Prince Rivers of Hamburg as a ringleader, an allegation that Rivers emphatically denied.

In a rare interview with an Atlanta journalist, Rivers intimated that whites were behind the calls for violence and his alleged involvement in the insurrection:

> *Gen. Joe Morris claims to have acted in concert, and under the instructions of Prince Rivers, of South Carolina. This potentate is a Major General of militia in South Carolina; served in the United States army as sergeant and color-bearer, has been Intendant of Hamburg, in that quiet old town across the river. As he occupied a conspicuous place in the public eye in connection with these occurrences, I decided to visit this sable generalship, and get what he had to say about the conspiracy. Accordingly, I took my*

way across the bridge in the early light of the morning, and found him at his house up stairs [sic] *over a store. He was not yet up, but on announcing my business I was ushered into a plainly furnished room, with pictures of Gen. Grant, President Lincoln, the famous surrender at Appomattox, and others of that sort, hanging on the walls. After a while he came in, a tall, somewhat slender black man, with a high forehead sloping back on the head, long and well combed moustache and beard, plainly dressed, about fifty years of age, a pretty good specimen in dress and appearance of a South Carolina planter's coachman before the war. He speaks with caution and deliberation, has no fluency, is evidently but poorly educated, and I should take him for a dark man in every sense of the word, dark in counsel and in deed. A man of that sort of coarse shrewdness peculiar to the negro, backed by more than ordinary obstinacy and force of natural character. I would not like to fall into his hands and be in his power. Judging from physiognomy he is a very cold-blooded cruel specimen of his race. He denied very strongly any knowledge of the troubles in Georgia, and said that he hardly knew Morris, that they would not recognize each othar* [sic] *if they were to meet on the street, so slight was the acquaintance. He says he has been invited to take part in processions, acting as marshal or general officer, in Georgia. But as to this particular matter he knew nothing of it. He had received an invitation under Morris' signature to attend a mass meeting to be composed of delegations, but as soon as he saw delegations to the call he knew he had nothing to do with it, and put it in his desk, where it is yet. He says further, that he was busy on his farm, and would not have attended any meeting at that time unless officially called to do so. He has never interfered in any way with Georgia affairs. All he wants is to be let alone in South Carolina. I told him his card of denial in the Constitutionalist might be accepted by the white people, but that his own color, as they were arrested, were constantly implicating him; could he explain that? To which he persistently replied that he did not know any of them, had never interfered in Georgia's affairs, and that not one of them could show a line that he had ever written on the subject. If they could, he was willing to stand convicted. He seemed to be a little excited as he proceeded and said he had no idea that any such letter as that alleged to have been found had ever been written by Candy Harris or any other negro. All that stuff about killing with axes and pitchforks, etc., was too absurd to be believed; the negroes, if they intended harm, would not issue orders in that kind of style. He intimated very strongly that it was written by some white person and dropped for the occasion, though he did not say so directly.*[178]

Chapter 8

Double Murder in Edgefield

As if conflict over drilling militias weren't enough, the grisly double murder of a well-to-do Edgefield couple and lynching of six Black men suspected in the killings shoved everyone to the edge.

John Harmon, seventy-five, and his wife, Catherine, fifty, lived on a plantation in northern Edgefield County, about twenty miles south of Greenwood. On the evening of May 17, 1876, their bodies were found on the bedroom floor with their heads beaten and throats slashed. Large pools of blood covered the floor. The murderer or murderers stole jewelry and weapons before trying to set the home ablaze.[179] It was a sensational story. Newspapers across the state covered the latest developments in amazing detail.

In the days that followed, authorities rounded up six Black men, two of them preachers. At a court appearance a week later, right after the indictment was read, two masked men threw a sheet over the sheriff. A white mob proceeded to usher the six defendants outside, where they were lynched. Gunfire exploded in the spring air as the mob fired more than one hundred shots over the course of twenty minutes.[180] A sympathetic Governor Daniel Chamberlain condemned the lynching and announced a $200 reward for the "arrest and delivery of any of the murderers of the six persons," although there's no evidence that anyone stepped forward to name the shooters, let alone collect any reward money.[181]

An uneasy quiet lingered in Edgefield and Aiken Counties until July 3, 1876, when Thomas Butler and some of Hamburg's Black residents exchanged some unflattering comments. Butler would later claim that the residents physically threatened him as he tried to ride through town. It's not entirely clear who started the verbal altercation, but hostilities spilled over into the next day, when Butler and Henry Getzen on the Fourth of July stumbled on the Black militia that Dock Adams captained in Hamburg.

On the surface, the July 3 altercation was relatively minor in the grand scheme of things, as was the right-of-way dispute that unfolded the following day. Recent events, however, proved that Hamburg had become a powder keg for a violent outburst of epic proportions.

Two years had lapsed since Ned Tennant, the flamboyant militia captain in Edgefield, drew ire from white southerners for drilling his guardsmen in public, leading to the First and Second Ned Tennant Riots. It also had been about two years since the Ridge Spring militia dustup and only six weeks since the double murder of John and Catherine Harmon and subsequent lynching of the African Americans suspected in their killings. Memories of these events and others no doubt flashed in Butler's and Getzen's minds as they contemplated what to do about the Hamburg militia.

Life on the Butler plantation had been chaotic, to say the least, with the family demonstrating a long history of violence and white supremacy. During the Civil War, Butler patriarch Robert J. Butler's claim to fame involved using his pack of hunting dogs to track down criminals, lost children and runaway slaves. It was a lucrative yet unsavory business.

Twice during the 1860s, the Butler home burned to the ground. Robert Butler also faced a murder charge after shooting a family enemy in a gun battle, but a jury acquitted him on the grounds that it was self-defense.[182] "This family of Butlers passed through some stormy periods and sustained some heavy losses in property, but their pluck and energy never succumbed to anything but death," one news report said.[183]

Thomas Butler was younger than his brother-in-law. Barely twenty-one years old, he was brash and easily agitated but also easily distracted and lazy. Thomas once remarked that he had "not been doing much business" after completing school. "I am just stopping around home, living with my father," he said.[184]

Thomas Butler wasn't very smart, either. He objected to relentless questioning of two Republican senators investigating the Hamburg Massacre. His inability to answer basic questions and follow instructions even irritated the committee's lone Democratic senator, who otherwise sided with the Butlers and other whites during a U.S. Senate inquiry months later.[185]

Thomas Butler followed in his father's footsteps. Years after confronting the Hamburg militia in 1876, the younger Butler hit the road to showcase the family's dog hunting skills. In 1879, Thomas Butler performed a "demonstration" of the family's special talent in the unlikeliest of places: New York City. Central Park, to be exact.

For a time, Butler's act was a hit. A troupe performing *Uncle Tom's Cabin* once offered him $150 per night for the purpose of using one of his dogs in a scene.[186] With slavery now abolished, the act helped Thomas monetize the family's dog hunting skills on the big stage. As part of the show, he would give a black preacher a head start before turning the dogs loose. Newspaper reports portrayed the show as being all in good fun. "The public must by no means entertain an idea that there is anght [*sic*] of cruelty to either man or beast in this unique entertainment, as the negro in question is devoted to his employer and hounds are well kept for."[187]

In later years, Thomas Butler was often seen skulking around Hamburg bars. It was in front of one of his favorite watering holes in Hamburg where he was involved in a shootout with a white hotel owner and his family. Butler, like his father, was tried for murder. And like his father, he was acquitted.

Henry Getzen was cut from a much different cloth. Raised by Reverend John Mealing, a local preacher who joined with whites during the Ned Tennant riots, Getzen joined the Butler family after marrying Thomas Butler's sister. He was twenty-six years old on July 4, 1876.

Getzen was much quieter than his boisterous brother-in-law but the more violent of the two white supremacists. He harbored a much deeper resentment for the freedmen of Hamburg and African Americans in general. Getzen's motivations were far more sinister. He played an integral role in the Hamburg Massacre, with some accounts stating that he personally executed at least two of the seven African Americans killed.

In Senate testimony given months later, Getzen had no qualms about publicly referring to African Americans as "niggers," something even his brother-in-law and father-in-law didn't do. As to the murder charges he faced for his role in the Hamburg Massacre, Getzen sounded almost blasé.

"What are you accused of in connection with the Hamburgh [*sic*] riot?" one senator asked.

"Well, sir, I don't know exactly what I'm accused of," Getzen replied.

"You are accused of murder, are you not?"

"I think I am accused of murder; I have forgotten now what the charges are against me," Getzen said. "I think it was murder. I think willful murder, if I'm not mistaken."

Getzen later admitted to being present for part of the Ellenton Riot, a massive racial clash that occurred later in 1876. It was about twelve miles as the crow flies from the Butler plantation to Ellenton, which begs the question of what Getzen was doing in Ellenton in the first place. Getzen never explained why.[188]

Sometime after the Hamburg and Ellenton riots, Getzen captured the attention of a U.S. marshal investigating voter intimidation. A warrant was even issued, although nothing apparently ever came of it, as Getzen went on to hold numerous public offices after 1876.

Farmers by trade, the Butlers often ferried goods back and forth between their plantation and Augusta. On busy days, the Butlers completed up to ten trips per day. When they weren't hauling brick, sand or manure, the Butlers sometimes took pleasure trips to Augusta.

They traveled the road so much that Robert J. Butler, the family patriarch, referred to Market Street as "my road." He spent between $150 and $200 per year on tolls to use Hamburg's roads and bridges. In Robert J. Butler's mind, Market Street was merely an extension of the Butler plantation, belonging to him.[189]

On July 4, 1876, when Thomas Butler and Henry Getzen turned onto Market Street and spotted an all-Black militia drilling two blocks ahead, they stared in disbelief. Dock Adams, a Georgia native who'd moved to Hamburg two years earlier, was its captain. About one hundred mostly Black residents lined the road, cheering the parading guardsmen.

Butler and Getzen would later tell the Senate committee investigating the Hamburg Massacre a slew of half-truths and bald-faced lies about Adams's demeanor before and during the drilling. To them, Dock Adams was no different than Ned Tennant, just another flamboyant Black man who dared to drill in the middle of their father's street.

The novelty of the drilling militia now fading, Butler and Getzen rolled their buggy forward toward the company.

Chapter 9

"This Is the Rut I Always Travel"

Getzen commanded the buggy forward, his horses trotting toward the Hamburg guardsman on an apparent collision course. The road was more than one 150 feet wide, weeds blanketing much of it, but not nearly enough to prevent horse-drawn buggies from easily passing through. "There was enough space for three or four trains of cars to pass on each side," Louis Schiller, one of the town's few white residents, later said.[190]

Dock Adams spotted the buggy almost immediately and knew that trouble was imminent. "They [Butler and Getzen] turned the corner and came up the street in a slow trot," Adams, the militia captain, recalled. "I saw that they intended to drive through the company, and I halted the company, and they stopped."

As they did, Adams walked toward the buggy. "Mr. Getzen, I do not know for what reason you treat me in this manner," Adams said.

"What?" Getzen blankly replied.

"Aiming to drive through my company, when you have room enough on the outside to drive in the road."

"Well, this is the rut I always travel," Getzen snarled.

"That may be true; but if ever you had a company out here I should not have treated you in this kind of manner," Adams said, his patience wearing thin. "I would have gone around and showed some respect to you."

"This is the rut that I always travel," Getzen repeated, adding, "and I don't intend to get out of it for no damned niggers."

At that point, when it appeared the two might come to blows, rain started to fall. Butler and Getzen later claimed that the rain is the only reason Adams allowed them to pass through without things turning physical. Adams said he was trying to defuse a rapidly escalating situation by giving in to Getzen's demand.[191]

Some of the militia grumbled as the buggy creaked through their ranks. The notion of caving to two white supremacists that spoiled their centennial celebration was nauseating. Among those voicing anger was Allen Attaway, the militia's vocal second lieutenant. Like Prince Rivers, the Hamburg trial justice, Attaway found new political and social opportunities after the Civil War. Attaway was among those winning election to Hamburg Town Council in 1871, joining Rivers and Louis Schiller. Attaway later served as an Aiken County commissioner, a post he still held in 1876.

Unlike Rivers, though, Attaway was outspoken, unfiltered even. This made him a polarizing figure, respected by his friends but also reviled by his enemies. Henry Sparnick, a white Republican who served as Aiken County probate judge, was a close ally of Attaway's. Sparnick described his friend as a man with "a great deal of resolution."

"His general reputation in that community was that he was a straightforward, truthful man; a man that could be depended on," Sparnick recalled. "I had a good deal of business negotiations with him from time to time on account of his relations to the county as one of its commissioners, and I always found him pleasant and affable, but a man of spirit."[192]

Attaway's spirit didn't sit well with most other whites, who found the very notion of Hamburg's Black residents entering politics repulsive—his candor making him an especially loathsome figure. White Democrats and African Americans intimidated into voting the Democratic ticket often spread false and defamatory stories about Attaway's character. In 1870, according to one account, Attaway was accused of voter fraud after an apparent attempt to remove ballot boxes from the courthouse.[193]

Another account accused Attaway of colluding with Jim Cook, the town's sheriff, to shake down travelers passing through Hamburg. John Lee later testified that Attaway and Cook took thirty-eight dollars from a man drinking from Ben Spring, although John Lee later acknowledged that most of his testimony was rooted in hearsay and secondhand accounts.[194]

Jerry Thornton Moore, an acquaintance living in nearby Beech Island, recalled how he often warned Attaway and Samuel Lee, another outspoken Hamburg resident, that it was only a matter of time before someone would try to kill them. "Look here, you are going to be killed. The white people are going to kill you," Moore said.

Attaway shrugged off the threat. "Tell me the man who said so and I will have him arrested," Attaway answered.

"I told Attaway and Lee what I had heard, that they were going to be killed, and they made light of it," Moore later recalled. "I heard that said in two months, twice, once in April and again in June."[195]

Adams, the militia captain, had a reputation too. Although it was Rivers who started the militia, it briefly disbanded; Adams reorganized it. Rivers remained its general in title, although Adams essentially called the shots.

The militia organized in 1870 and incorporated by the state legislature in 1872. Rivers, named the militia's first captain in 1873, was a short time later promoted. Rivers was succeeded first by John Williams, who in turn was succeeded by Dock Adams, who was elected captain in November 1873, although due to a paperwork error Adams wasn't officially commissioned by the state.[196]

In 1874, the state reorganized all of its militias, including Hamburg's. Adams was a noncommissioned officer, but the Hamburg militia elected him captain anyway. Louis Schiller, a white Jewish newspaperman and Hamburg town councilman, served as the company's secretary.[197]

But Adams was also headstrong, often coming across as disrespectful and defiant, especially to whites, who wasted no time smearing his name. In Augusta, where Adams spent most of his adult life, his enemies characterized him as a "great rascal" and a "common street loafer" who was seen "loafing about the courthouse."[198]

Even Samuel Spencer, an African American resident of Hamburg and influential cotton factor, was lukewarm at best when asked to describe Adams's character. "It is thought that there is better men than Doc [*sic*]; his reputation is not very good," Spencer said.[199] Rivers had held his own captain in contempt over how he conducted himself in court.

However, John Williams, colonel of the militia, thought Adams had "a very good reputation in Hamburgh [*sic*]; also in Augusta," where Adams had captained a militia in Augusta called the Grant Guard.[200]

As for Butler and Getzen, there was no confusion over how they regarded Adams. They'd seen enough of him and his Black militia drilling on "their street." To them, Dock Adams was another Ned Tennant, another Black militia captain preparing for war with the whites.

Butler and Getzen would later claim that the militia spotted their buggy and, in response, positioned themselves so as to block their path. They testified that the militia retreated to Ben Spring, the well in the center of Market Street, and occupied the left half of the road. A shallow ditch ran across the right half. Sidewalk to sidewalk, the road spanned at least 150 feet, half the length of a football field. The militia occupied less than one-third of it. "There was no bridge across the ditch, and they deployed across the street in this position with their guns across their shoulders, [indicating] and they asked me was I going to try to drive over them," Butler stated. "I told them no; all I wanted was the road."[201]

Butler and Getzen would also claim that a boy beat a drum under their horse's head in an apparent attempt to excite the steed. In the meantime, Adams and other members of the militia taunted them, they said. "No by God, you can't go through here," Adams allegedly said. Then it started to rain. "By God, if it didn't rain we would keep you here all night, but it is raining and I will give it up," Adams continued.[202]

At that moment, the militia split ranks, and Butler and Getzen drove through. Schiller, the militia's secretary, had been closely watching the verbal confrontation. He summoned Sheriff Cook, who made a futile attempt to stop Butler's buggy. The brothers-in-law ignored Cook's cries as their buggy made the slow climb to Butler's plantation.[203]

Robert J. Butler, the Butler family patriarch, was furious. The following day, he traveled down to Hamburg to swear out a complaint against Adams.

The hearing was set for July 6 at noon, a Thursday.[204]

Chapter 10

The Trial of Dock Adams

On the morning of July 6, 1876, a small entourage consisting of Tommy Butler, Harrison Butler and their father, Robert; Henry Getzen and his uncle, J.P. Mealing; and Dr. H.A. Shaw trekked down the hill from the Butler Plantation to Hamburg for the hearing. Dock Adams and Allen Attaway from the militia were already there, as was Prince Rivers in his capacity as town judge.

Also on hand was Henry Sparnick, the county's probate judge, as an observer. Sparnick had been in Hamburg on personal business that day when he caught wind of a trial in which Rivers was presiding. When Sparnick learned that the trial involved his good friend Attaway and, by extension, the Black militia, Sparnick went to the courthouse, where a large crowd had already assembled. Outside, Attaway approached Sparnick and asked if he would represent him and other members of the militia, who had been charged with obstructing the right of way. Sparnick agreed. He examined the summons and immediately regarded it as illegitimate. "It was very defective. It was not a legal paper; it was not even a summons," Sparnick recalled.[205]

A native of Charleston and Republican to the core, Sparnick led a prolific career in South Carolina, both as a politician and a newsman. His earliest record of service was in October 1865, when he was in consideration for being appointed reading clerk to the South Carolina legislature.[206] By 1870, Sparnick was practicing law in Richland County and also serving on the board of regents for the state insane asylum.[207]

Sparnick eventually moved to Aiken County, where he was elected probate judge in 1871. He was a Republican delegate to the 1874 Congressional Convention and a railroad company director and even launched his own newspaper, a weekly Republican publication called the *Aiken Tribune*.[208] "He [Sparnick] made a fine local reputation for himself as a newspaper man, wielded a ready pen, and made the *Tribune* a sparkling paper. Its circulation was never large, as there were comparatively few reading Republicans in the county."[209]

Some supporters floated his name as a possible Congressional candidate: "Why is it that that Congressional District doesn't take up a man like Henry Sparnick, the editor of the *Aiken Tribune*, one with a name worthy and respectable at once? He might have some weight in Congress; certainly is it that he would not make his constituents ashamed of their representative."[210]

But Sparnick also had baggage. In May 1876, the state tried him for misconduct in office after he was indicted for converting estate money for personal use. The first trial ended with a hung jury, but he was later convicted and paid restitution to settle the matter.

The *Courier-Journal*, a Democratic newspaper in Aiken and a fierce critic of Sparnick and his newspaper, gleefully pontificated about Sparnick's guilt. When the first trial ended in a mistrial, the *Courier-Journal* protested the inclusion of nine African Americans on the twelve-man jury.[211]

Sparnick often turned the other cheek to the *Courier-Journal*'s smear campaign, although one time in 1874 he did respond with a rare rebuke. Calling the *Journal*'s editor "pusillanimous," Sparnick challenged the newspaper to validate its circulation and advertising numbers. According to the wager, the loser would pay the difference "in equal proportions to the treasury of the several churches in Aiken, on Christmas Day, to be expended by them amongst the poor of the town."

"Now, *Courier-Journal*, put up or shut up!" Sparnick demanded.[212] There is no further record of whether or not the *Courier-Journal* accepted the challenge and, if so, who won the wager.

Sparnick injecting himself into the Hamburg trial didn't sit well with other whites on hand. Robert J. Butler was outraged, expressing a "great deal of indignation" over Sparnick's presence. "He [Robert J. Butler] said that he was not advised that there were to be attorneys there, and that he had none himself, and asked for a postponement of the case," Sparnick said.

Later, Sparnick tried to convince the elder Butler to drop the matter. He explained that there was no merit to the complaint and that a higher court would overturn it. "I asked him to abandon the prosecution; that even if he did get a judgment, that it was a matter of appeal, and if it went up to a higher court, it would not stand there a minute."

Sparnick was probably correct that the summons was not legally binding. And a higher court likely would've overturned any judgment, assuming the case ever made it that far. Butler, however, could care less. In his view, these African Americans had obstructed "his road" and had meddled with his family. He was determined to make them pay. "He said he would do no such thing; that the negroes of Hamburg had been very offensive; that they had interfered with his son and son-in-law on the 4th of July; and he was determined that they should be punished," Sparnick said.

Butler then issued a foreboding claim that he'd bring a large group of twenty-five to thirty men with him to Hamburg. "Mr. Butler, perhaps there will be two or three hundred," Sparnick replied, half serious but also somewhat alarmed.

"Well, yes, damn it, two or three thousand," Butler boasted.[213]

Butler later claimed he would've been willing to drop the matter. All he said he wanted was an apology. "I told him [Sparnick] if they would come forward and say that they had done wrong, and if they would not interfere with the road anymore, I would have no more to do with it," Butler said. "He went off and promised to come back, but did not come back at all."[214]

Butler backed off his postponement request after Adams offered to represent the guardsmen pro se. Sparnick agreed, although he stood ready to file an appeal if necessary. Attaway formally announced that Sparnick had withdrawn as counsel, and the hearing began. Any hope that Sparnick's withdrawal might cool tensions fizzled almost immediately.

Getzen was the first witness, and since Adams was acting without legal representation, Rivers allowed him to cross-examine Getzen directly. Matters quickly spiraled out of control. Adams made Getzen look almost foolish on the stand, which both helped and hurt his cause. Through a series of irrefutable questions, Adams systematically picked apart Getzen's narrative that undisciplined, impudent Black militiamen had improperly blocked the road. But the pugnacious nature in which Adams asked his questions infuriated the pro-Butler crowd.

"Mr. Getzen, did I treat you with any disrespect when I spoke to you or didn't I treat you politely?" Adams asked with his opening question.

"I can't say that you treated me with any disrespect, but I can say this much, that there was one or two members of the company that showed some impudence to me, and also I saw them load their guns," Getzen replied.

"Mr. Getzen, didn't you see me examining the cartridge boxes and also the pockets of the members of the company to see if they had any ammunition, before they went on drill?"

"Yes." Getzen admitted.

"Did you see any?" Adams pressed.

"No I didn't."

"Didn't you know that I found one man with a cartridge in his pocket and I took it away from him and scolded him about it?" Adams asked.

"Yes."

"Well then, are you certain that these men loaded their guns?"

"I saw them move their guns and I thought they loaded," Getzen replied, his patience wearing thin.

Rivers also started losing his patience with Adams's line of questioning. In Rivers's mind, it had exceeded the bounds of judicial decorum. Adams, disdainful of the proceedings, came across as sarcastic and disrespectful.

Robert J. Butler claimed that Adams's conduct "was so bad before the court," but he couldn't state with any specificity what Adams said or did that irritated him. "He asked him [Getzen] a good many questions, but I do not recollect the questions that he asked," Butler said.

Reverend J.P. Mealing, Getzen's adopted father, claimed that Adams actually seemed to be questioning him vicariously through Getzen. Mealing later said that Adams cursed the court for several minutes as he was being arrested.

Dr. H.A. Shaw, an Edgefield physician and family friend, said the questions that Adams asked were "irrelevant."[215] Getzen claimed, without offering evidence or citing examples, that Adams was insulting and "used very bad language," something a newspaper report later claimed. "Damn Rivers and his court; while I have a company no [*sic*] one damn negro or white man shall rule me," Adams purportedly said.[216]

Regardless of the exact circumstances, and after first admonishing Adams, Rivers ruled the militia captain in contempt and suspended the proceedings. The hearing was continued to July 8, a Saturday, at 4:00 p.m.[217]

Attaway fumed. Belligerent and combative, he allegedly called Rivers a "white livered son of a bitch," within earshot of the departing judge, and that he would "wade in blood up to his [knees]." Mealing claimed that Attaway threatened to kill the next white man who tried to prevent the militia from drilling. "I carry no arms, but we have got arms," Attaway said, according to Mealing. "The white men have ruled the black men long enough."[218]

An affidavit would further claim that Attaway threatened whites with violence. "He said he was ready for the white men to come on, and the next one that tried to stop his company he would see that no report was made of it, as he would shoot them so clean that there would be nothing in their mouths to tell."[219]

Meanwhile, Robert J. Butler summoned General M.C. Butler (no relation) from Edgefield to intercede. General Butler had extensive experience dealing with drilling militias, namely, Ned Tennant's militia. It was General Butler who stood up to the Edgefield militia, and it was that man Robert J. Butler wanted in Hamburg.

Back at Rivers's house on the afternoon of July 8, 1876, there wasn't much Rivers could say or do to convince Adams to reappear in court. It was impossible to ignore the bands of rifle club members, also known as "red shirts," descending on Hamburg. Armed to the teeth, they were itching for a fight.

Years later, at a rally in Edgefield County, former U.S. Senator Ben Tillman recalled the scene with nostalgia and glee. "The purpose of our visit to Hamburg was to strike terror, and the next morning when the negroes who had fled to the swamp returned to the town, the ghastly sight which met them of seven dead negroes lying stark and stiff certainly had its effect," Tillman said.[220]

Chapter 11

General Butler Arrives in Hamburg

It was about 3:00 p.m. when General M.C. Butler rode into Hamburg on July 8, 1876. Butler's "official" reason for being there was to serve as an attorney in the right-of-way dispute between two white men and the town's all-Black militia. In actuality, he was determined to disarm the Hamburg militia, just as he had done with Ned Tennant, the flamboyant Edgefield militia captain. White rifle clubs and Black militias had been clashing with increasing frequency, and he was going to put a stop to the drilling. "Now, by God, I want those guns, and I'll be God damned if I ain't going to have them," Butler later said.[221]

Barely two years had passed since General Butler had brought down Ned Tennant, elevating his status as a hero among the state's rifle clubs. The first rifle club formed in Charleston in 1869, supposedly as a social group that would gather together for target practice. The real purpose of rifle clubs, though, was to target African Americans, and Black militias in particular.[222]

To General Butler, the Hamburg situation was déjà vu. He'd disarmed Ned Tennant because the concept of an armed militia was unpalatable. Rallying rifle clubs worked in bringing down Tennant, and Butler thought that the same would happen in Hamburg.

From Butler's perspective, Hamburg was antithetical to his genteel southern upbringing. He found the town's tattered buildings and weed-infested streets to be repulsive. Hamburg was hardly a place a man of Butler's distinguished lineage would visit. General Butler had descended from a long line of prestigious military and political figures. His paternal grandfather William Butler served during the American Revolution as well as the War of 1812, achieving the rank of major general. William Butler also served thirteen years in Congress, as did William Butler Jr., his son and General Butler's father.

Commodore Matthew Calbraith Perry (for whom General Butler was named) and Commodore Oliver Hazard Perry, both heroes during the War of 1812, were Butler's uncles by marriage. He also was the nephew of Andrew Pickens Butler, a former U.S. senator, and also of Pierce Mason Butler, a former South Carolina governor. General Butler was born to lead.

In Butler's youth, he was "Captain in all out door [*sic*] sports, fair but full of mischief and fun." Before heading off to college in 1854, one of Butler's instructors predicted that the future Civil War general "will be a great leader of men," noting that "[c]hildhood shows the man as morning shows the day."[223]

In June 1863, as a colonel at the Battle of Brandy Station, a cannonball maimed Butler's leg, and he wound up losing it. As he bled on the battlefield at Brandy Station, he reportedly ordered troops to tend to other wounded soldiers, including the mortally wounded Captain William Downs Farley, who risked being crushed by a collapsing horse. "Go at once to Farley," Butler ordered. "He needs you more than I do." After the battle, he gained promotions to brigadier general and then to major general.

Rivaling Butler's nobility as a commander was a veiled ruthlessness he occasionally unleashed on his enemies. Butler was front and center in the hunt for Ned Tennant in 1875. His house had been burned to the ground, and while Tennant was the lead suspect, the evidence against him was purely circumstantial. That didn't stop Butler from leading hordes of vigilantes against Tennant.[224]

The following year, after his election to the U.S. Senate in 1876, Butler found himself at the center of a political coup d'état in Washington, D.C. Republican political operatives tried to frame the Edgefield senator for infidelity and then publicly slander his name. Butler, though, caught wind of the scheme and hatched his own plan to embarrass and intimidate the conspirators.

James Morris Morgan, a former Confederate soldier and a Butler colleague, described the general turned senator in this fashion:

> *General Butler was an extraordinarily handsome man—tall and graceful, and possessed of the manners of a Chesterfield. In the hour of danger he was one of the coolest men I ever saw, and he feared neither man nor devil.*

But with all of his beautiful manners, when he wanted to, he could be the most cold-blooded, insolent human being that mortal eyes ever beheld.

The Republican plan was elaborate. It involved dispatching a woman of the demimonde class to meet Butler while he was alone at his Washington, D.C., home. Once she was in place, Republican operatives would barge in moments later to "catch Butler in the act." The ensuing political scandal would discredit Butler and possibly end his political career since women of the demimonde had a reputation for sexual promiscuity.

Upon learning of the plot, Butler asked Morgan to join him at his home. The woman arrived as expected but was shocked to find two men inside. Rattled, she tried to leave through the front door, but Butler and Morgan blocked her path. They then hinted that police might become involved if she didn't quietly leave through the back door. She promptly departed.

A short time later, when the Republican operatives showed up as planned, there was no demimonde. Only Butler and Morgan were inside. Butler unleashed the full fury of his rage at the shocked radicals. "General Butler was hopping about on one crutch while making most menacing flourishes in the air with the other," Morgan recalled. "The general was the possessor of a most highly sulphurated vocabulary when his angry passions were aroused, and he was using it with unstinted prodigality."[225]

The same sort of "sulphurated" vocabulary stewed in Butler's head as he headed toward the office of Prince Rivers. Accompanying Butler were Robert J. Butler and Henry Getzen. Inside Rivers's office, General Butler spotted William Nelson, the town's constable. His feet perched on the desk, Nelson was fanning himself on the blazing hot July day. Butler took Nelson's casualness as a sign of disrespect.

"Where is Rivers?" the general snarled.

"Mr. Rivers is at his house, I reckon, but he will be here directly," Nelson answered.

"Go and tell him to come here to me," Butler demanded.

Nelson pushed back. Unfazed and unafraid, he reminded Butler that the hearing wasn't until 4:00 p.m. "I am not Mr. Rivers' office boy; I am a constable, and I am here tending to my business. He won't come any quicker by my going after him."

This only irritated Butler further. First he demanded that Nelson bring him paper and a pen, which Nelson refused. "Come in, sir, and sit at the table," Nelson said.

Butler then leaped from his buggy and entered the office. Getzen, visibly armed and staring at Nelson in a "resenting manner," followed Butler inside. Butler demanded a chair, which Nelson initially refused to provide.

"There's a chair," he said.

"God damn you, give me the chair you are sitting on."

Realizing he was greatly outnumbered and outgunned, Nelson capitulated. "All right, if this chair suits you better than the other, take it," he replied.

Now fuming, Butler unleashed a series of obscenities and racial slurs. "You God damned leather-headed son of a bitch, you, sitting down there fanning yourself, God damn you," Butler exclaimed. "You God damned son of a bitch, you want to have a hole put through you before you can move."

A third man, also armed, entered the office. Getzen raised his gun and pointed it directly at Nelson. As he did, Robert Butler ran into the office with a pistol. Thomas Butler was still sitting on his horse outside, also armed. Robert Butler demanded that Nelson leave to find Rivers. "God damn you, this God damned drilling has got to stop. I want you to go for Rivers," General Butler said.

Nelson again refused. "I have no right to go for Rivers, and I am not going," he said.

After more threats and cursing, the men departed and regrouped at George Damm's grocery store. Nelson remained at the courthouse until Rivers arrived. As 4:00 p.m. approached, more groups of armed men amassed outside Damm's store. He would later estimate the crowd at between seventy-five and one hundred, most of them armed with pistols, sixteen-shooters and revolvers.[226]

Chapter 12

Last Chance for Peace

Armed whites continued pouring into Hamburg. Many were drinking or already drunk, creating a toxic stew of hate, bellicosity and inebriation. Dock Adams topped the list of men they wanted to kill. "They were getting drunk very fast, or drinking liquor and appearing like they were drunk, and saying they were going to kill every God damned nigger in Hamburgh [*sic*] that day, especially Dock Adams," Adams recalled.

Following Adams on this hit list was Allen Attaway, the militia's outspoken second lieutenant and county commissioner. Attaway had accompanied Adams to see Prince Rivers but was even more adamant about not attending the hearing, fearing for his safety. Others on the hit list included Jim Cook, the town sheriff; David Phillips, the militiaman who Thomas Butler claimed threatened him; and Louis Schiller, the town's Jewish newspaperman and militia secretary.

Given the growing likelihood of armed conflict, Rivers resigned himself to the reality that Adams and his officers would not show up for court. He knew that convincing them otherwise would be futile. "I shall go to court at the usual time. Your name, of course, will be called, and if you don't answer to your name—well you won't be there. That is all; you won't be there to answer," Rivers said.[227]

As violence escalated toward inevitability, some militia sympathizers pieced together last-ditch peace feelers. Henry Sparnick, the county's probate judge, and Samuel Spencer, an African American resident of Hamburg who ran a successful cotton factory, worked independently to broker a peaceful resolution.

Sparnick fancied himself as a man of influence with both Black Republicans and hard-core Democrats like General M.C. Butler. He arranged for Adams, Attaway and other militia leaders to meet Butler at George Damm's grocery story a few blocks away. Spencer also met with Butler, who agreed to meet with the militia leaders.

Adams was willing to go, but Attaway thought it was merely a diversion so the whites could ambush them. "Well, there is no one more readier to settle it than I am," Adams said. But as Adams looked toward Damm's store, right away he spotted throngs of men outside. He noticed them drinking as well. Adams was still willing to meet Butler, but before agreeing to do so, he asked Spencer to see if Butler would be willing to meet at Spencer's house. Butler agreed. They were supposed to meet at 5:00 p.m., but when 5:00 p.m. arrived, Butler changed his mind. Now he wanted to meet the militia leaders outside of town hall.

Meanwhile, Sparnick and Spencer continued acting as intermediaries, hoping that both sides could reach a resolution. When Sparnick asked Butler what it would take to settle the matter, Butler's reply was blunt. "Well I think it would be necessary for them to apologize to my cousin and surrender their arms," Butler responded.[228]

"Suppose these negotiations or these propositions fail, will it be likely that there will be a collision?" Sparnick asked. Butler replied in the affirmative. "Well, as I am one of a few white radicals here, if a collision takes place I suppose I will stand a pretty poor chance?" Sparnick asked, half serious. But Butler remained stoic and steadfast.

"I have no doubt that you will." Butler said blankly.[229]

Meanwhile, Spencer pleaded with the militia members to meet General Butler, but he was unsuccessful. Butler didn't take kindly to the news. His patience wearing thin, the general didn't care about the militia's fears. It was now 5:00 p.m., and Butler was growing weary of the back and forth. "Sam, there is not any use in parleying any longer. Now, by God, I want those guns, and I'll be God damned if I ain't going to have them," Butler exclaimed.[230]

Furious, Butler drove his buggy across the river to Augusta, where he remained for about thirty minutes before returning to Hamburg. Adams took refuge in the Sibley Building, a two-story structure one block from the river that served as the militia's armory. About forty men, mostly militia members and a few private citizens, sought shelter there as well.

When Butler returned to Hamburg, he met with John Gardner, the town's intendant, who made his own last-ditch effort to reach a settlement. For a third time, Butler said that the only terms he would accept were the unconditional surrender of the militia and its arms. Butler then informed Gardner that he had fifteen minutes to get the town's women and children to safety.[231]

Rivers offered to collect the guns himself and ship them to Daniel Chamberlain, the state's Republican governor. Butler balked. "Damn the governor. I am here as General Butler," he said. "By God, you had better go and do something. There is going to be hell to pay here if them guns and officers ain't delivered."[232]

In Butler's version of events, he verified that he agreed to discuss a possible settlement with the militia leaders but also claimed that they kept giving him the runaround. In the meantime, a crowd of Hamburg residents taunted him while he waited at Damm's store, Butler claimed. "These colored people would pass this door that I was in and hawk at me and scrape their feet on the sidewalk, and do a great many things that were disgusting," he said. "But I had made up my mind not to get into a bad humor about it, and took no notice of it."[233]

Butler acknowledged that he suggested the militia should surrender its arms, but only inasmuch that doing so might help prevent a violent conflict. He also said that Rivers sought what was a fourth attempt to reach a settlement. "General, if these people will give up their arms and send them off, what security have you to offer? Will you guarantee their safety down to Columbia?"

Butler said he could make no promises but surmised the militia leaders would be safe if they complied. "I have no doubt that there will not be any trouble," he said. "But if you want security, I take it that there are ten or twenty of the best men in Aiken County who will be security for these arms until they are deposited in the State arsenal, where they belong."[234]

In any event, Adams rejected Butler's ultimatum. He said that the arms belonged to the state, and it was only to the state that the arms could be legally surrendered.[235] Adams later said he would agree to surrender the arms to Rivers since he was the militia's general, but he was uncharacteristically deferential. "No, I don't demand them. I have no right to do it. You must use your own discretion about it," Rivers said.

As the time approached 6:00 p.m., Adams and Butler exchanged notes. Adams repeated his position that he had no authority to surrender arms to a private citizen. In reply, Butler wrote in no uncertain terms that Adams had one last chance to surrender. "I want them guns, and by God, I have got to have them," Butler declared. "I will give you half an hour to give up the guns."[236]

Adams stood his ground. "I told him, well, then he would have to take them by force, and then I would not be responsible for them," he said. Butler expected—hoped, perhaps—that this would be the result.

During the Ned Tennant riots of 1874 and 1875, Butler had led groups of rifle club members against Tennant and his militia. Both times, he'd secured the surrender of Tennant and his followers. But Butler's success came at a cost, namely the loss of his home to fire, which he no doubt blamed on the militias. Angered by the Hamburg militia's defiance, Butler terminated further negotiations. He promptly ordered the deployment of the white forces that had been gathering in Hamburg throughout the day.

About seventy-five yards from the armory, along the Savannah River, about two dozen men on horseback fanned out along the embankment. Some men on foot took positions by a nearby railroad trestle, while others assembled behind a large tree. A fourth group took position in the street, some camouflaging themselves in the grass.[237] The remaining men guarded the town's main entry and exit points like "pickets."

"I could see him [Butler] placing men all around town," Adams recalled.[238]

The militia was surrounded. Butler's forces totaled about two hundred, outnumbering the militia and other bystanders in the armory five to one. There was no way in or out of Hamburg, a town now under siege. After a few minutes, someone shot a signal gun by the river. Then the first rifle blasts crackled in the air.

The Hamburg Massacre had begun.[239]

Chapter 13

The Hamburg Massacre

The first gunshots came from somewhere along the Savannah River. There, a group of well-armed whites sheltering on an embankment sprayed the Sibley Building with bullets. More gunmen flanking the armory up on the street poured fire into the two-story structure as well.

Nobody was shot in the opening barrage, although one bullet whizzed by the head of William Nelson, the town's constable, as he watched the volley from the roof of the Sibley Building. "There was a little gutter there, I suppose about two feet wide, and the ball just came right through the gutter right by me," Nelson recalled.[240]

When the shooting began, fear drove some residents still caught outside to seek shelter in the Sibley Building. One of those men was Frank Robinson, a nineteen-year-old corporal in the Hamburg militia. Robinson spent the day working in a local store, where he noticed the droves of rifle clubbers amassing in town. Some of them came into the store looking to buy cartridges and ammunition. Under instructions from his boss, Robinson refused to sell them any ammo. In response, the white men cursed and threatened the teenager and then left the store. "You are one of the damned scoundrels that belongs to the militia company," one of the men said.[241]

Also caught in the attack was Spencer Harris, who arrived in Hamburg less than an hour before the shooting commenced. He later fled the drill room for what he thought would be a safer hiding spot—underneath his house.[242] Louis Schiller, the Jewish town councilman, fled to a neighbor's house, a decision that probably saved his life.

Back at the armory, the men gathered inside temporarily found adequate protection. The building's brick walls repelled most of the bullets pelting the two-story structure. Some bullets pierced the windows, sending jagged glass shards crashing to the ground. The shooting persisted off and on for about thirty minutes. In that time, the militia held its fire.[243]

Thomas McKie Meriwether. *Edgefield Advertiser*, February 23, 1916.

Outside, a brash young man by the name of Thomas McKie Meriwether was among those shooting from the embankment. His parents described the twenty-three-year-old as possessing the "easy manners of a country gentleman," although Meriwether's words during the massacre illustrated otherwise. "We're going to kill every God damned nigger that there was in Hamburg, and then I'm going to try the women and children. After I get through with them, I will go up away and try Old Jesus Christ."[244]

Meriwether's boast would soon be put to the test. Earlier that day, he had traveled to Augusta to conduct business on his father's behalf. As he rode Salem, his horse described as "a small sized dark bay stallion," across the river, two Black ferrymen spoke of an impending clash between the militia and the whites. Concerned that the Black militia "was defying the white man's country," Meriwether armed himself with two pistols and rendezvoused with his father, Joseph Meriwether, along the Savannah River. They stood under the last abutment of the railroad bridge. "Here, papa, take these and let me have the rifle," Thomas Meriwether pleaded.[245]

Meriwether fired with such fervor that his gun overheated, so he set his rifle down against a nearby railroad trestle. Impatient for it to sufficiently cool so he could resume killing radicals, Meriwether never saw the bullet screaming from behind, entering the back of his head "directly above the [occipital]." A shower of red sprang from his forehead like a shooting geyser as the projectile carved a tunnel through his brain. Meriwether staggered a few steps, his arm flailing along the stone wall, leaving "the mark of a bloody hand where it slipped on the abutment." Then he fell, a pool of blood forming around him. Death was virtually instantaneous.[246]

Nobody knows from which gun the fatal shot was fired. Regardless, the shooting resumed with a fury few had seen since on the battlefield. Amid the hail of gunfire, a group of men carried Meriwether's lifeless body across the river to Augusta.[247]

The impact of Meriwether's death on the rifle clubbers served as a rallying call for every white in Hamburg. It was at this point that General Butler would later say that the bloodthirsty mob was drunk and already well beyond his control.[248]

Ben Tillman, a future governor, senator and Sweetwater Sabre Club member, said that Meriwether's killing galvanized the white gunmen. "If the white men were determined when they began that bloody business, this sad and unexpected death added ten-fold fury to their feelings," Tillman recalled.[249]

The firing continued for the next thirty minutes, continuing into nightfall. An unusually bright full moon illuminated the warzone unfolding below. The tips of rifles crackled like exploding fireworks. Smoke billowed into the air.

As the firing continued, Adams climbed onto the roof to survey the scene outside. There was a momentary lull in the firing as an unidentified voice started barking orders. "Go over the river and get two kegs of powder. We're going to blow that building up!" the man exclaimed.

Adams knew that time was running out. If the voice was correct, the white mob would soon blast the armory into pieces, and those who survived would be sitting ducks for the bloodthirsty rioters. The only hope for survival was to escape.

Luckily, the vigilantes outside never stationed anyone behind the building, giving the militia an escape route through a set of second-story windows. It was also pitch black behind the building, which would further aid in their escape. "In the back part of the yard there was no firing. Everything was perfectly still," Adams recalled.

A carpenter by trade, Adams devised an ingenious escape plan. Repurposing lumber from the drill room interior, Adams built a makeshift ladder that his men could use to sneak out the unguarded second-story windows.

At first the plan worked perfectly. Adams ordered Attaway and most of the other occupants to escape through the back windows and wait. Adams would remain behind for a short time to provide cover fire as a diversion. "I told him [Attaway] to go down first and receive all the men that were in the building, and keep them together till I came out," Adams said. "I would stay up there with two or three men, and every once in a while fire and make them think we were in the building, while they were escaping."[250]

When it came time for Adams to depart, a new problem arose. Adams and the remaining militia had reached the second-story windows when he realized that Attaway vanished. Overcome with fear, the outspoken politician panicked and fled, as did many others. Only about fifteen men under Attaway's watch remained behind. Meanwhile, the white mob was intensifying in both size and fervor. Droves of armed whites poured across the river from Augusta. Adams's plan was falling apart. The only hope, Adam thought, was to head north on Market Street. "Men, we are surrounded," Adams flatly stated. "I don't know how we will get out of here. There is but one way. You will have to fight pretty rapidly to get out that way."

It didn't take long for the mob to notice some of the fleeing men. Harrison Butler, the elder son of Robert J. Butler, spotted them first and sounded the alarm. "Here they come!" Butler shouted.

By now, the men who had departed for Augusta to fetch a cannon had returned with their secret weapon. Later, news reports would state that someone pried open a gate at the Washington Artillery and stole an iron centennial six-pounder cannon. The company's captain that possessed the cannon claimed no knowledge of the theft, saying that "he had previously stated to several gentlemen that if a request was made to him for the cannon, he would not grant it."

Back in Hamburg, as the whites moved in and with the cannon trained on the armory, Adams led his men into the streets and fought their way out of town. Miraculously, nobody was killed, although one of Adams's officers was shot in the leg. It was at this point that the cannon opened fire on the armory. The blast was deafening, with the opening salvo sending more than a dozen egg-shaped balls hurtling into the drill room.[251]

Boom! The cannon fired again. Then it fired a third time. And then a fourth. The whites jeered with each firing of the cannon. Even though the militia's armory had already been evacuated, and even though news accounts later said that the damage was mainly superficial, blasting the building with shells made for good theater.[252]

As the inebriated mob jeered a symbolic victory, Adams's detachment was making its way up the hill toward Robert J. Butler's cornfields, the one place where the mob never thought to look. His men safe for the moment, Adams made his way back to Hamburg hoping to rescue any stragglers.

The trip back to Hamburg was perilous. It was now approaching 10:00 p.m., and a glowing full moon hovered in the night sky, radiating light on Hamburg. The unusually bright moon made hiding from the mob nearly impossible. Adams estimated that he was shot at more than two hundred times. He found a few of his men hiding under houses, although almost nobody was willing to come out for fear of being captured.

Not long after returning to Hamburg, Adams spotted a man running into the street. He called to him, but the fleeing man, later identified as Jim Cook, the town's sheriff, ignored Adams and kept running. Adams quickly realized that groups of white men were hunting Cook. Men positioned on both sides of the street opened fire, turning it into a no man's land for anyone unlucky enough to be caught in the crossfire. Miraculously, not one bullet struck Cook, and equally as amazing, nobody else was hurt. But Cook was quickly captured by Henry Getzen, Ben Tillman and a handful of other whites who surrounded the town's sheriff.

"I've got the son of a bitch," one of the whites bragged.

"God damn you! We have got you," another man said. "You have been town marshal here, going about here arresting democrats, but you won't arrest any more after tonight."

Adams slid back into a nearby cornfield, realizing that there was nothing he could do for the doomed sheriff. Standing in the shadow of a cornstalk, Adams watched helplessly as Cook begged for mercy. "Mr. Getzen, I know you and will ask you to save my life. I haven't done anything to you. I have only done my duty as town marshal."

But there was no mercy—only the cold stoicism for which Getzen was known. What's more, Getzen had been charged with developing the white mob's hit list. Cook's reputation for allegedly targeting whites traveling through Hamburg made him a prime target. "God damn you, your knowing me ain't nothing. I don't care anything about your marshalship. We are going to kill you," Getzen replied.[253]

At that moment, the gang members raised their rifles and opened fire. "Oh Lord! Oh Lord!" Cook cried as bullets pummeled his body and shredded his face, drenching his body in blood. An affidavit later said that Getzen, Thomas Butler and Thomas Butler's brother, Harrison, fired the fatal shots.

"You call on the Lord you son of a bitch," a voice responded coldly.[254]

Years later, Tillman recalled that Cook "tumbled in a heap almost turning a somersault." He also noted that a member of the mob struck a match near Cook's mutilated face to verify his identity. His identity confirmed, the gunmen removed Cook's boots and stole his watch as trophies, fitting retribution in their minds for the sheriff's alleged shakedowns and thievery.[255]

The novelty of killing Cook fading, the mob turned its attention to the cornfield in which Adams was hiding. Sensing this, Adams slipped away and ducked into the home of Louis Schiller, the Jewish newspaperman, whom the gunmen were chasing through the swamps.

Adams hid in Schiller's home for about an hour before some gunman arrived, looking for Schiller. Again Adams managed to avoid capture, slipping out the back door as men barged through front door and ransacked the house. A similar scene was unfolding at Adams's residence, where whites looted his home and destroyed everything else they couldn't take. Powerless to stop them, Adams fled Schiller's property.

"Halt!" The authoritative scream sent shivers down Adams's spine. He thought for sure this time he'd been discovered. Adams turned his head and spotted Robert J. Butler running out of a nearby store, rifle in hand. Only it wasn't Adams whom Butler had spotted. Butler's attention was focused elsewhere.[256]

Moses Parks, a member of the militia, and William Nelson, the town's constable whose casual demeanor had irked General Butler, had fled from the armory for the dimly lit backyard of Lafayette Davis, a Hamburg merchant sympathetic to the African Americans.

Parks led the way as he and Nelson crossed Davis's yard, hurdled a cross fence and scrambled toward the street. Nelson gazed at the glowing full moon in the cloudless sky, lamenting that it didn't bode well for their survival chances. "The moon was shining as bright as day. I thought it was mighty bright, and I would have liked if it was dark," Nelson recalled.

Robert J. Butler's shrieks immediately captured the attention of other gunmen, who zeroed in on Parks and Nelson. The commotion quickly captured the attention of Davis. He pleaded with the gunmen to halt their advance, but his pleas fell on deaf ears.

"Who is that?" Davis asked.

Nelson retreated into Davis's yard and hid behind a brick outhouse until daybreak. Parks kept running.

"There goes a God damned nigger!" Robert J. Butler announced.

"Don't shoot! Don't shoot!" Davis pleaded.

Bam! *Bam*!

"There goes a God damned nigger!" More shots echoed in the nighttime air. "There goes one of the God damned sons of bitches."[257]

Another shot fired. This time the bullet found its mark, and Parks fell to the ground, the fatal shot fired by Robert J. Butler. The hunter had found his prey. "God damn him! I have got him," Butler boasted.

Three men were now dead, two of them Black residents of Hamburg. Not wishing to become a casualty himself, Adams fled again. This time he sought shelter inside the home of the town's postmaster. He went to the second floor, where he had a perfect vantage point of General Butler and the white mob. It was the perfect vantage point of the "dead ring."[258]

Chapter 14

The Dead Ring

As the crowd of white men ransacked Hamburg, they rounded up as many of the town's Black population as they could find. Many residents hid in their homes and, in some cases, under their homes. The crowd found them anyway and ushered them to the "dead ring."

The dead ring was aptly named. In a grassy field along the Savannah River and near the South Carolina Railroad, General Butler's men encircled the African Americans who weren't killed on sight when hostilities erupted. There the twenty-one men who'd been rounded up waited with baited breath while a coalition of racist whites mulled who would live or die.

Some of the whites wanted to mow down the entire group in a blizzard of gunfire and be done with it. Others merely wanted to arrest them. In the end, General Butler ordered a "court-martial." Butler assembled a kangaroo court that devised a list of men the mob would kill.[259]

One of the men detained was Harry Mays, a former slave who lived next door to Prince Rivers. Mays had the misfortune of being home as the whites pillaged his neighbor's house. As they broke into his home, Mays slipped out the back door, only to encounter more gunmen. About a dozen men waiting outside spotted Mays on the back porch.

"Come down, you damned big son of a bitch!" they hollered.

"I haven't done nothing," Mays insisted.

"None of you haven't done nothing," the mob replied.

One of the men taken to the dead ring was Nelder John Parker. A corporal in the Hamburg militia, he was known colloquially and in the local press as John Thomas.[260] He never made it to the ring, however. Just before Thomas reached the ring, two Augustans known only as "Twiggs" and "Chaffee" begged the mob not to hurt the Hamburg resident. At that point, General Butler said something peculiar. "Are you one of the damned rascals?" Butler asked.

When Thomas answered affirmatively, someone shot him in the back. General Butler later claimed to condemn the shooting in the strongest possible terms. Before any more shots were fired, Twiggs and Chaffee threatened to shoot anyone who fired again at Thomas. They then carried the bleeding corporal across the river to Augusta. The gunshot left Thomas critically wounded, and he died in the days that followed.[261]

One newspaper, however, claimed that Thomas survived the shooting. Weeks after the Hamburg Massacre, the *Courier-Journal*, a fiercely Democratic newspaper in Aiken, claimed without offering evidence or citation that Thomas survived the shooting and "has sufficiently recovered to be able to go to work."[262]

The *Courier-Journal*'s callous claim is indicative of most news reports during Reconstruction. Often times, General Butler and the rifle clubbers were regarded as heroes who liberated South Carolina from Republican rule. As for African Americans, most newspapers portrayed them as instigators who got what they deserved. That's how it was with John Thomas. In the days that followed the Hamburg Massacre, most newspapers portrayed him as a gun-toting outlaw looking for a fight. It was a tenuous argument at best.

At an arraignment hearing weeks later, a railroad watchman said that hours before the shooting began, an armed Thomas said to him that Dock Adams had been arrested and that "the boys were not going to allow him to be tried."[263]

Also taken to the dead ring was Allen Attaway, the militia's second lieutenant. Like many of those captured, Attaway fled the armory in a state of panic when the crowd trained the cannon on the armory. Finding Attaway was a top priority for the whites. They loathed the loudmouthed county commissioner, his pugnacious nature notwithstanding. He also held public office and was a ranking officer in the Hamburg militia, making Attaway a prime target—and he knew it.

"Mays, what do you think of this?" Attaway asked.

"I don't know, Attaway, what do you think of it?"

"Do you think they will kill any of us?"

"Yes, I do think so," Mays said grimly.

"Do you think they will kill me?" Attaway asked.

"I do," Mays replied. "All you have got to do now is to pray to God to save your soul. Just give up your wife and children and everything else, for they are going to kill you."

At that moment, Attaway hung his head and sobbed. He didn't say another word until the whites returned and started taunting him.[264] "You are the magistrate, I suppose. You is [*sic*] a damned nice looking magistrate. We will fix you, we are going to kill you tonight, sure, without a doubt."

"Gentlemen, I am not ready to die, and I ain't did anything to be killed. Please let me pray," Attaway begged.[265] But Attaway's pleas were futile.

"Damn you, you ought to have been praying before now. You have talked enough without praying. We is going to kill you."

Attaway continued to beg when Henry Getzen approached. "Attaway, is that you, old fellow?" Getzen asked, not bothering to hide his cruel cynicism. "Damn you, we will fix you directly."

"O, Getzen! Getzen!" Attaway cried.

"What do you want from me?" Getzen responded dismissively.

"Do all you can for me!"

"Yes, God damn you, I will do all I can for you. I will do it in a short while. I will fix you now in a short while, damn you," Getzen barked before marching off.

A few minutes passed, and then a familiar voice shouted. "Allen Attaway!" General Butler blurted.[266]

At that moment, Getzen, Thomas Butler and at least two other men returned to the dead ring. They grabbed Attaway, who then uttered his final words. "Gentleman, I am not prepared for death," Attaway said.

"I don't care," Getzen replied.

"Will you allow me to prepare to meet my God?" Attaway asked desperately.

"I don't care, we are going to kill you," Getzen repeated.

Getzen, Butler and the others ushered Attaway across the railroad tracks and into a small oat field. The group disappeared over a hill, and then rifle blasts echoed in the air.[267] That was the last time anyone saw Attaway alive. A coroner's inquest noted that he'd been struck by four bullets, one of them to the brain. Death was instantaneous. His body was found the following morning in the oat field, mutilated by angry whites seeking an extra measure of revenge. "After he was dead the brutes in human shape struck him over the head with their guns and stabbed him in the face with their bayonets."[268]

The nineteenth-century historian John Chapman of Edgefield County offered an even more ghastly account of what happened to Attaway. "The

Radicals say that the tongue of Attaway, which had been used so badly, was cut out," Chapman said. "Of the truth of this statement this deponent saith not."[269]

Defeated and disgusted, Dave Phillips turned to the others in the ring. It was Phillips whom Thomas Butler claimed had threatened him earlier in the week. "What is all you begging so? If they are going to kill us all anyhow, what is the use of us begging so?" Perhaps Phillips knew that he was next. Sure enough, his name was called. In contrast to Attaway, Phillips seemed resigned to his fate. The whites led Phillips over the same hill as Attaway and executed him.

"Dave got up just like a soldier," Mays recalled. "He looked like he didn't care no more for it than he would about eating, and he walked right along. I heard the guns fire, and they came back, but Dave didn't come."

"Pompey Curry!" Curry also belonged to the militia. Using the element of surprise, Curry took off running at the urging of his cousin Mays. The impromptu strategy momentarily caught the white mob off guard. "Pompey jumped and ran, and they shot at him several times, and they said that they had done killed him," John Freyer, the militia's first corporal, recalled. "We supposed that Pompey must have got killed in running. They said that they had killed him, and they all burst out laughing."[270]

In reality, Curry did not suffer life-threatening injuries. An attorney general report confirmed that a bullet struck his right leg below the knee.[271] Curry's escape also proved vital in identifying the co-conspirators. Even Ben Tillman acknowledged years later that Curry was a "star witness," who was able to implicate Tillman and others as direct participants in the Hamburg Massacre.[272]

"Hamp Stevens!…Albert Minyard [Myniart]!" One at a time, Stevens and Myniart were led across the railroad tracks. Stevens was a large mulatto man. "O, gentlemen I haven't done nothing," Stevens said with futility.[273]

Small and sickly, Myniart kept quiet, hoping to go unnoticed. It was only through process of elimination that Myniart was discovered. Only after everyone else had been identified did Myniart acknowledge his true identity. "Get up from here, we have been hunting for you," one of the whites ordered.[274]

Initially, there was some disagreement over whether or not to kill Myniart. At least one of the whites almost seemed to take pity on him. "O, let that boy alone. He is sick."

The majority, however, wasn't moved. "O, God damn him, we'll fix him too."

The whites led Myniart across the railroad tracks and shot him. Myniart survived a few hours but succumbed to his injuries after sunrise. "I saw him after he was killed, and I saw where they had cut off a big piece of meat off his rump," Mays recalled. "This Albert Myniart boy had a great big piece of flesh cut off his rump, just chopped off with a hatchet or something," Mays continued. "Then he was cut in his side here, chopped right between his ribs with a hatchet."[275]

Unlike the others killed in the Hamburg Massacre, neither Stevens nor Myniart belonged to the militia. They didn't appear to overtly express any political allegiances, either.

Dock Adams surmised that they were targeted because of an unspecified business dispute they had with a man known only as Lamar. As for the others, their murders were acts of intimidation meant to reassert white authority and reestablish Democratic control in government. "These others were killed down there simply because they were leading Republicans, and also belonged to that company," Adams said.[276]

By the time the Hamburg Massacre ended, eight men had been killed, seven of them African American. Five others had been wounded, four of them African American.[277]

The mob, however, never tracked down Adams. General Butler considered the militia captain to be Public Enemy No. 1. It was Adams who led the Black militia and who challenged two white men of privilege. It was also Adams who embarrassed Henry Getzen in open court. And it was Adams who ordered the militia to shoot at the rifle clubbers, killing young Meriwether. Much to the mob's chagrin, Adams gave them the slip.

"God damn it! Can't you find that Dock Adams? We want to get him," one man demanded.

"We'll have him before day," another man said.

Others weren't willing to wait. "Well, we had better go to work and kill all the niggers we have got. We won't be able to find that son of a bitch [Adams]." Adams remained hidden for several hours until the crowd dispersed. Once the streets cleared, he boarded a train for Aiken. Aside from occasional clandestine trips to Hamburg to check in on his family, Adams avoided returning home for fear of assassination.[278]

William Nelson, the town's constable, who had evaded capture by hiding behind an outhouse in Lafayette Davis's yard, wandered the streets of Hamburg in a daze. The unenviable task of identifying the victims fell to him, as did preparation of their coffins.[279]

As for the gunmen, they reassembled at Ben Spring, the drinking well in town, from which they gleefully drank without fear of being fined. The mob had seen to that hours earlier with the murder of Jim Cook. Afterward, those who didn't go home headed over to Henry Getzen's home to feast on watermelon after what they considered a "momentous and strenuous day's work."[280]

Their "work" continued into Sunday as a squadron of men consisting of Robert J. Butler; his eldest son, Harrison Butler; and Getzen continued searching for Louis Schiller, the Jewish newspaper publisher and secretary of the militia. Schiller had hidden within his home Saturday night and throughout the day Sunday. A fellow Jew by the name of Davis Lepfield implored for Schiller to leave lest he be captured. "They are determined to have you. They say you are in the house, and that they are going to take you out of here," Lepfield told his friend.

Schiller's wife insisted that he flee as well. After sunset on Sunday, he made his way to the railroad and walked three miles to the east toward Storm Branch. Along the way, he encountered Robert J. Butler, Harrison Butler and Getzen. As they cocked their rifles and trained them on Schiller, he ducked into a nearby swamp. Butler grabbed his hounds to hunt for Schiller as he had hunted for escaped slaves before the war.

Schiller remained on the run for days, and at one point, Butler and his dogs came within two hundred yards of him. Somehow Schiller managed to stay one step ahead, but not before getting turned around. He circled back to his home in Hamburg, where he shaved his mustache to disguise his identity. On Thursday, he boarded a train for Columbia after successfully sneaking away.[281]

Chapter 15

Aftermath of a Massacre

As the men responsible for slaughtering seven African Americans gorged on watermelon and slept, Albert Myniart lay bleeding in the street, weeping for help. It was about 5:00 a.m., and the dying militiaman "feebly" asked for some water. A few bystanders brought him water to drink and placed him on a mattress. He died a few hours later.

Not long after onlookers were tending to Myniart, the wife of Allen Attaway wailed uncontrollably at the sight of her husband's mutilated body. Bystanders later moved Allen Attaway's body back into his home, out of public view. The rest of the dead were relocated to Hamburg Town Council chambers. Hundreds of bystanders—some relatives and others merely curious—gathered to catch a glimpse of the aftermath. Some wept but most remained silent. Jim Cook. Moses Parks. Allen Attaway. Dave Phillips. Hamp Stevens. Albert Myniart. They were all dead, slain by white supremacists a few hours earlier.[282]

By daybreak, Constable William Nelson heard the wails of widows as he was walking through the streets of Hamburg. It was now Nelson's responsibility to prepare coffins for the six slain men. Sheriff Cook, his former boss, was among them. Barely twelve hours had passed since Nelson and Parks had sprinted into the moonlit street, where they stumbled into an ambush. Nelson escaped, but Parks wasn't so lucky. A posse led by Robert J. Butler opened fire, killing Parks, who had the misfortune of leading the way.[283]

Some semblance of justice tried to emerge in the following months. A week after the massacre, on July 15, 1876, the clerk to the U.S. House of Representatives spent the first twenty minutes of the session reading a letter from an unidentified eyewitness to the Hamburg Massacre. The gripping letter retold with chilling accuracy the events from that infamous night:

> *The United States Government is not powerless, and surely she will not be silent in an emergency like this, the parallel of which pen cannot describe. In this Centennial year, will she stand idly by and see her soil stained with the blood of defenseless citizens, and witness the bitter tears of women and children falling upon the murdered bodies of their loved ones?*[284]

Entering the letter into the record was Representative Robert Smalls (R-Beaufort), one of the most prominent nineteenth-century African Americans ever to serve in the U.S. House of Representatives. Appalled by the killings, Smalls leveraged outrage over the massacre in an attempt to block a Democratic-supported measure to send South Carolina militia to reinforce U.S. troops deployed to the Texas frontier.

The Smalls amendment stirred fierce partisan debate, with Democrats denigrating Hamburg and its Black population while Republicans voiced sympathy for the victims. Among the notable Republicans in Hamburg's corner was a forty-six-year-old House veteran by the name of James A. Garfield. By 1881, he would become the nation's twentieth president.

The Ohio Republican said that the Hamburg killings occurred "without warrant or authority," noting that the Hamburg militia was legally organized and legally empowered to carry arms, despite claims from General Butler and most House Democrats. "We fought a great war to establish the Union and the equal rights of citizens before the law," Garfield said. "I wish we could lay aside all the bitterness of that contest….When that is done, we can shake hands in full assurance of peace, and can hang the olive branch over all our doors."[285]

It was an idealistic message, a message shunned by the whites back in Aiken and Edgefield Counties. While Washington was awash in outrage, General Butler and his acolytes received the royal treatment. Locals serenaded the white supremacists, hailing them as heroes as they triumphantly rode their horses into Aiken.

In August 1876, a little more than one month after the Hamburg Massacre, a flotilla of men facing charges for their respective roles embarked from Graniteville, where they "surrendered" to the county sheriff and slowly proceeded up the hill to Aiken for their bond hearings. General Butler led the way. An estimated "5,000 mounted men from all parts of Western Carolina" lined the street, many of them wearing red shirts symbolizing

James A. Garfield. *Courtesy Library of Congress, Prints and Photographs Division, Washington, D.C.*

the rifle clubs to which many of the defendants belonged. Women waved handkerchiefs adoringly.[286]

The impromptu parade began around 11:00 a.m., with everyone riding in pairs in what quickly became a major spectacle. Men rode straight into the center of downtown Aiken, assembling in front of Lyceum Hall, a two-story wooden structure on Laurens Street that housed the town's courthouse.[287] "To say that the town was on tiptoe of expectation concerning the events of the day would be but faintly to express the sentiment of the very large crowd of people who had come from miles around to witness the proceedings," the *Anderson Intelligencer* reported. "The appearance of the men was very imposing, and although all appeared in good spirits, the best order was maintained, the only demonstration being a spontaneous shout from the assembled crowd as the men rode up."

Aiken media described the arrival with even greater adulation: "Never before…had so respectable a band of prisoners as those Aiken and Edgefield gentlemen, of all ages and conditions, who come filing into town mounted on well-conditioned, mettlesome steeds to give bail for their appearances at the September term."[288]

Judge John Maher, who presided over the hearings, set bond at $1,000 for each of the men charged, knowing full well the futility of cracking down on the Hamburg ringleaders. "I cannot imprison an entire community, and they have their rights, which will be respected," Maher said. "You will make no triumph of this matter, but give your bail and go quietly to your homes."[289]

If by saying "make no triumph," Maher meant "stay out of trouble," his words fell on deaf ears. Most notably, Henry Getzen and Ben Tillman took up arms one month later in the Ellenton Riot, where at least one hundred African Americans were killed in three days. Neither faced any real consequences.[290]

Defending the Hamburg participants in court was Daniel Sullivan Henderson, an Aiken attorney. No friend to African Americans himself, Henderson orchestrated the exoneration of not only General Butler, Ben Tillman and other Hamburg Massacre ringleaders but also those accused a few months later of killing African Americans in the much bloodier Ellenton Riots:

> *During the troublous campaign of 1876, when South Carolina was redeemed from the disgraceful rule of ignorant, illiterate native whites, half savage negroes, aliens, and a general combination of thieves, young Henderson came to the front as a leader in the struggle for white supremacy, honesty, and decency.*[291]

For his part, General Butler peppered newspapers with lengthy editorials that spun a masterful tale of how he had no foreknowledge of the troubles in Hamburg. He said he only came to Hamburg in a professional capacity. Butler claimed, without evidence and based solely on hearsay, that the militia planned to lynch Thomas Butler and Henry Getzen if the court wouldn't convict them. General Butler further denied going to Augusta to recruit gunmen or secure a cannon. He also denied leading the assault against the militia and disavowed any involvement in the execution of those taken captive:

> *During the firing, some parties unknown to me brought over a piece of artillery, and fired four or five times at the building and returned. The firing of the negroes from their position then ceased. I left the crowd arresting the negroes. How many were killed or how they were killed I do not know.*

DECLARATION OF EQUALITY.—Justice "Five more Wanted."

Hamburg Massacre cartoon. One of many Thomas Nast cartoons calling attention to the Hamburg Massacre shortly after a white mob executed seven African Americans. *"The 'Bloody Shirt' Reformed," courtesy Library of Congress, Prints and Photographs Division, Washington, D.C.*

Denying involvement, Butler did not condemn the violence either. "This collision was the culmination of the system of insulting and outraging white people, which the negroes had adopted there for several years," Butler added. "Many things were done on this terrible night which, of course, cannot be justified, but the negroes 'sowed the wind and reaped the whirlwind.'"[292]

Between Hamburg and Ellenton, race riots escalated in South Carolina. In Washington, with no apparent end in sight to the bitter partisanship between Republicans and Democrats, the U.S. Senate appointed a special committee to investigate the Hamburg and Ellenton riots, as well as voter intimidation in general.

Dubbed the "South Carolina Committee," the three-person panel interviewed nearly two hundred witnesses in December 1876 and January 1877. Republicans held a majority on the committee. In the end, while no additional charges were filed, the panel published a voluminous, three-volume report spanning more than two thousand pages that serves as one of the most detailed accounts of the Hamburg Massacre.

Senator Angus Cameron (R-Wisconsin) chaired the subcommittee. He'd only been in office a year after eking out a one-vote victory for a post he never sought, but he accepted it to prevent the seat from falling into Democratic hands.[293]

Senator Isaac P. Christiancy of Michigan, the subcommittee's other Republican, was the panel's eldest member at age sixty-four. A highly regarded Michigan Supreme Court justice, Christiancy was content to remain on the bench, where he had served with distinction since 1857. "From the time Justice Christiancy came to the court, until the year 1875, he steadily grew in learning ability, and he ranked well with the ablest of his great colleagues," a judicial colleague wrote.

As a legislator, however, Christiancy's career never gained traction. A domestic scandal involving a spouse who coerced him into marriage under threat of litigation further marred his political career. He resigned in 1879.[294]

Rounding out the trio was the pugnacious Senator Augustus Summerfield Merrimon, a Democrat from Asheville, North Carolina. In 1878, the *New York Times* castigated Merrimon for unfulfilled promises and political duplicity, saying that he portrayed himself as a liberal Republican to curry favor with moderate voters:

> *Like all Southern "Independents," his first care after he succeeded in getting his seat was to prove to the country he was "in every respect a true and loyal Democrat." He forgot all his promises, repudiated his obligations, turned his*

> *back on the men without whose aid he could not have been elected, and was soon recognized as one of the bitterest Democratic partisans in Congress.*[295]

During the Hamburg inquiry, Merrimon more than lived up to his reputation. Snarky and narrow-minded, he routinely placed the blame squarely on the militia and town leaders, viewing Hamburg as a lawless shantytown ruled by corrupt, inept politicians. "It is alleged before this committee that the Hamburg riot grew out of political considerations…there was a state of lawless misrule there," Merrimon said. "A set of desperate negroes occupied the town. They paraded its streets with guns, which they allege were militia guns."

"The condition of things there had become intolerable. They were often carrying on hostile controversies among themselves," Merrimon continued. "This, I insist, is an important fact to be shown, with a view to reflecting light upon the circumstances that brought about that riot."[296]

Local newspapers sided with Merrimon. They decried the hearings as biased and rigged. One report complained that 75 percent of witnesses were either African Americans or Republican sympathizers. The report claimed that Senators Cameron and Christiancy stuffed the hearings with an "elaborate and exhaustive collection of outrages, atrocities and horrors."[297]

Another report, in trying to exonerate General Butler, made the outlandish claim that Republicans, acting at the behest of Governor Daniel Chamberlain, engineered the Hamburg Massacre:

> *The Hamburg Massacre was concocted and forced to consummation by political leaders most trusted in the counsels of Chamberlain.…The Hamburg outbreak was one of the deliberately planned features of the Chamberlain political campaign to arouse the country, furnish an excuse to place South Carolina under marshal law* [sic], *and thus ensure a new lease of carpet-bag power in the state.*[298]

Such lunacy was commonplace at the time. The spate of fake news reports didn't stop the Senate hearings, however. Testimony continued over a one-month period, ending in mid-January 1877. If not for the South Carolina Committee, there likely wouldn't be a full and truthful account of the Hamburg Massacre.

It's worth noting that Prince Rivers, perhaps one of the most crucial figures in this sad story, never testified. His only real commentary came in an affidavit from South Carolina attorney general William Stone's final report.

As Rivers recalled, General Butler requested a short delay in the 4:00 p.m. hearing that was scheduled for July 8. He promised to return an hour later but never did, instead crossing the river into Augusta. Butler returned with two companies of soldiers and demanded that the militia immediately surrender its arms. When the militia refused, it was General Butler who ordered the white mob to open fire on the armory, Rivers said. "Butler told me he would have the arms or burn the town. I, Rivers, offered to box the guns and send them to Chamberlain, but Butler would not agree to this."[299]

Sadly, the town's trial justice so admired during the Civil War by his commanding officer wouldn't be much more help to the militia. His home was one of many the white mob ransacked on the night of the massacre, stealing anything of value and destroying the rest.

In November 1876, Democrat Wade Hampton III "defeated" Chamberlain, owing largely to ballot box stuffing and voter intimidation. This placed the election results in dispute, and with support from federal troops, Chamberlain remained in office for a few more months.

For Rivers, this only delayed the inevitable. He became a lame duck trial justice, his tenure only guaranteed as long as Chamberlain remained in office. Once Hampton's election became official, Rivers's dismissal became a virtual certainty. Pressure for his resignation mounted. A hit piece authored by a Charleston reporter based in Augusta painted a dreary image of Rivers's courtroom, portraying it as an "ill ventilated apartment." Jurors were "ignorant, unkempt and uncomely fellows, one among them being an ex-convict, whom I recognized on sight, and another was sound asleep," he wrote. "The whole proceeding was simply and exceedingly childish, and the result obtained, if any, was utterly worthless as regards [to] the nature and amount of testimony elicited," the reporter continued.[300]

The Aiken newspaper took a similar stance in an op-ed piece published months later:

> *P.R. Rivers and Frank Arnim, two bogus Trial Justices of Hamburg, are exercising the privileges of such office in direct defiance to the mandates of Gov. Hampton. We advise our country men to pay no regard to their summons, or any process from them or their officers. Their game is to fine every one convicted before them, knowing Sheriff Holley will not recognize them. We suppose they will pocket all fines. Good thing for them if they are allowed to continue.*[301]

Chapter 16

DEMOCRATS DISSOLVE HAMBURG

Wade Hampton didn't take office until April 1877. By June, the former Confederate general had officially dismissed Prince Rivers as Hamburg trial justice, although Rivers's ouster was only the beginning of his legal difficulties. As the summer of 1878 drew to a close, a pair of peculiar scandals plagued Rivers for years.

The first involved dozens of congressmen who accepted bribes in exchange for voting for the Blue Ridge Railroad scrip bill. Newspapers published an exhaustive three-part series about the affair that involved more than $72,000 in bribes. Rivers "admitted" in an affidavit to participating by accepting $500, while also noting that state lawmakers routinely accepted such bribes. "Other members were there, coming in and going out in the same way as in the payment heretofore mentioned above. There were so many men I can hardly specify which of them that I met; they were in such a crowd."[302]

Another scandal purporting to involve Rivers and other members of a commission charged with acquiring property for a new Aiken County Courthouse. The commission identified the Gregg Mansion in Aiken County for this purpose, acquiring it for $15,000. The only problem is that the property was actually worth $10,000, with some unofficial appraisals pegging the value at $8,000. An indictment claimed that Rivers and others conspired to divvy the difference among themselves, according to an indictment.

There were numerous curiosities relating to the timing of the cases. The Rivers affidavit was published on September 5, 1878, the day after his indictment in the Blue Ridge Railroad bribery case. Both scandals stemmed from activity allegedly occurring in 1871, seven years in the past, raising statute of limitations issues. Defending or disproving the allegations would have been exceedingly difficult for anyone. But for African Americans in a state run by white southern Democrats, the likelihood of prevailing was virtually impossible.

In February 1879, an Aiken County court convicted Rivers on one count, although the jury recommended him "to the mercy of the court." He appealed to the state Supreme Court, although the case never resurfaced.[303]

As it turns out, General Butler engineered a deal between the federal government and South Carolina Democrats. In exchange for not prosecuting any of the Hamburg killers, the federal government agreed to quietly drop corruption cases brought against Republicans.[304] Thus, the case against Rivers was dropped, though not until 1885. By this time, Rivers had moved to Aiken, where he spent his remaining years in relative obscurity working as a coach driver and "trusted employee" of the Highland Park Hotel, where he was often spotted "attired in his livery suit and tall beaver hat." He spent his final eight months confined to bed, suffering from an unspecified illness. Prince Rivers died in April 1887 and was buried, at his request, at Randolph Cemetery in Columbia.

In an obituary, the *Aiken Journal and Review* generally noted that Rivers led a distinguished career and was "respected by the white people and looked up to by his colored brethren with much reverence" but also noted that he "was far above the average darkey."[305]

Other Hamburg participants and sympathizers also found themselves in legal difficulty during the final years of Reconstruction. Among them was Henry Sparnick, the white Republican and former Aiken County probate judge who aided the African Americans in Hamburg.

It was around 6:00 p.m. on July 8, 1876—the day of the Hamburg Massacre—when Sparnick boarded the last train departing Hamburg, missing the hostilities by a few hours. In the months that followed, he continued to claim Aiken as his residence, although owing to political heat, he spent no more than a few days there through December. By 1877, the Republican newspaper Sparnick operated had folded and he had moved out of state. "The [Wade] Hampton regime ran him out of town and the paper ceased publication," according to one account.[306]

In January 1877, Sparnick gladly offered testimony to the South Carolina Committee, giving the three-member panel a detailed account of what occurred leading up to the Hamburg Massacre. His transparency and cooperation came back to haunt him though. Later in 1877, Sparnick's misconduct in office charge from the previous year just happened to resurface. An Aiken County jury convicted him in absentia in September of appropriating $2,700 from an estate to his personal use.[307]

By the time of his sentencing, Sparnick had already vacated South Carolina, although curiously, his sentence was never made public. The local press, relying on anonymous sourcing and no proof, claimed that Sparnick's sentence remained under seal. Referring to him as the "notorious Henry Sparnick," the *Aiken Journal*, which had been a fierce business competitor of the *Aiken Tribune* paper he operated, said the former probate judge who had "plundered the widows and orphans of Aiken County" was spotted doing business in Chicago. "Sparnick was a man of brains and education, but was actually the vilest of the infamous gang who held high carnival of crime during the radical regime," the *Aiken Journal* reported. "A sealed sentence awaits him in the Clerk of Court's office…which will be opened whenever he makes it convenient to visit South Carolina."[308]

But Sparnick never returned. Ostracized in South Carolina, Sparnick found success in Colorado, where in his later years he clerked for a judge in Denver. He also served as editor of a newspaper called the *Tribune*. In Colorado, at least, Sparnick "was well known and greatly liked throughout the entire state."[309]

Sparnick lived his remaining years in the Mile High City until his death on November 29, 1885. His remains were transported via train to his hometown of Charleston, where he was buried the following year. However, vindication for the "notorious carpetbagger" would have to wait several more years.

In 1892, a successor of the *Aiken Journal*, the same newspaper that had excoriated Sparnick in life, retroactively walked back some of its accusations against the former probate judge. Through his good graces, the newspaper wrote, Sparnick had made amends with the victims his enemies claimed he had swindled. Unsurprisingly, the *Journal and Review* was conspicuously silent about the sealed sentence that supposedly awaited him. "To his credit, so we have been informed, that several years after his departure, he compromised with the parties whose money he had used by paying about sixty per cent of his indebtedness, and in turn was given a clear receipt."[310]

The *Journal and Review* further remarked that Sparnick was a man "of remarkable ability" who cultivated a "fine local reputation" in Aiken County.

It was a fine tribute, albeit seven years tardy. "He…wielded a ready pen, and made the [*Aiken*] *Tribune* a sparkling paper. Its circulation was never large, as there were comparatively few reading Republicans in the county. The *Tribune* flourished about six years, and during this time, was the official organ of the Republican Party. It went up with its party in 1877, and its editor, Henry Sparnick, sought a more congenial clime in the wilds of the far West."

Dock Adams disappeared into relative obscurity after Hamburg as well. In the months following the massacre, Adams kept a low profile, traveling to Hamburg only when necessary to care for his ill wife and also to find work. But Hamburg grew increasingly dangerous for African Americans, who were threatened by whites virtually every day leading up to the 1876 elections in November, so Adams limited his trips there. "It has been usually expressed that they were going to kill out all the radicals, and all those that didn't vote the Democratic ticket they would kill," Adams recalled.

In subsequent years, Hamburg became an even more dangerous place. Henry Getzen, one of the chief instigators of the violence, had become the town's trial justice by 1878. Adams didn't hide his feelings about Getzen. "This Getzen is the prime leader of all the difficulties and crowds that have been brought in there since the Hamburg riot," Adams said.[311]

Deciding that Hamburg was just too dangerous, Adams moved to Charleston, where he worked as a watchman and also held various positions under Republican leaders. At one point, he was named chairman of the Charleston Republican Club.

Wade Hampton III, first South Carolina governor after Reconstruction. *Courtesy Library of Congress, Prints and Photographs Division, Washington, D.C.*

Adams lived a "comparatively quiet life" until his death in September 1898 at the age of sixty-two. But unlike Sparnick, Adams remained a chief antagonist of the Hamburg Massacre in the eyes of whites. A newspaper obituary claimed, without evidence, that Adams also participated in the Ellenton massacre and that "it was he who kept the Negroes constantly worked up and he is responsible for many of their lives being taken."[312]

As for Hamburg, with its leadership gutted and common citizens scared into submission, African American rule was nearing its end. In April 1877, President Rutherford B. Hayes removed the remaining federal troops stationed in South Carolina, ending Reconstruction and facilitating the Democratic rise to power. Wade Hampton III officially assumed the governorship, and without Chamberlain in Columbia to offer political protection, Hampton officially dismissed Rivers from office on June 1, 1877. Days later, the state launched efforts to strip Hamburg of its town charter.

A group of thirty-one intrepid Hamburg residents petitioned the state in a last-ditch effort to save the town:

> *To the Honorable the President and Speaker of the House of Representatives of the State of South Carolina, the memorial of the undersigned most respectfully Showeth that the Undersigned Citizens and Tax Payers of the Town of Hamburg, S.C. do hereby Protest against the repeal of the Charter of the Said town for the following reasons to wit.*
>
> *1st We have a good governor and in the Town of Hamburg South Carolina, and we firmly believe that they will protect our rights as citizens and Tax Payers.*
>
> *2nd We have reason to believe that certain party or parties have some movement on foot to attempt through Your Honorable Body to deprive the citizens and Tax Payers of the Town of Hamburg, SC of their Charter.*
>
> *Hopefully Your Honorable Body will give Petitioners a just and favorable consideration and your Petitioners ever pray.*[313]

On June 9, 1877, Hampton formally signed a bill repealing the town's charter, revoking with a stroke of a pen that which Henry Shultz so assiduously lobbied for fifty-four years earlier. One Upstate South Carolina newspaper summed it up this way: "This will break up one of the foulest nests of scoundrels that ever disgraced civilization, and prevent any recurrence of the Hamburg Riot."[314]

Chapter 17

Democrats Rise to Power

Not long after the Hamburg Massacre, southern Democrats swiftly rose to power. Voter intimidation, media manipulation and backroom deals allowed men guilty of murder to land cushy political appointments—men like General Butler, Ben Tillman and Henry Getzen.

Butler's political rise became a virtual certainty. Heralded as a hero, the Democrats now controlling the state legislature appointed him U.S. senator, a post he held for two decades. An 1882 biographical sketch had this to say about Butler:

> *General Butler is likely to be a leader in South Carolina politics for many years to come, and conspicuous in the sessions of the Senate of the United States, by reason of his ability, his personal attractions, and his gentlemanly bearing. He is a church communicant, happy in his domestic relations, and blameless in character, however in any of his habits of thought and feeling acquired under the shadow of the "peculiar institution" he may antagonize those of the citizens of the Northern States.*[315]

Butler served until 1894, when he faced a tough challenge from another ringleader of the Hamburg Massacre and rising star in the Democratic Party.

Benjamin "Pitchfork" Tillman was a fearsome figure, both verbally and physically. He lost his left eye in his youth when heat from a pine torch burned his socket, causing a tumor. The resulting disfigurement was permanent and only added to his imposing appearance. A contemporary observed that Tillman's "countenance is singularly coarse" and that "there is not a more formidable figure to be found in America." His head, "with an air of defiance," was almost "Napoleonic" in its stature. "The face makes one think of piracy, cannibalism. It is the splendid outline of the head that redeems and explains it. Not that there is any trace of cunning or treachery in the countenance; yet it is beyond comparison as an example of savage masculinity."[316]

Tillman's caustic persona propelled him to the governor's office in 1890. When his gubernatorial opponent challenged his lack of Civil War service at a debate, Tillman unleashed a verbal onslaught that converted the decidedly anti-Tillman audience into his camp. "As for your insinuations of cowardice and lack of patriotism, I spit them out at you, and spurn you and them with contempt," Tillman shouted.[317]

As governor, Tillman took many actions directly impacting Hamburg, including a crackdown on animal fighting. An 1887 law banning cockfighting didn't stop the bloodsport from continuing. Four years later, the *Augusta Chronicle* published several stories about cat, dog and chicken fights flourishing in Hamburg, arousing public outrage. The fights had been organized by interests from North Carolina and South Carolina.

Tillman was enraged, not so much over the barbarism of animal fights, but rather by the optics. He saw animal fighting as backward and unrefined, a stain on South Carolina's integrity that the governor sought to stamp out. He couldn't stand the thought of disgracing South Carolina in the eyes of the nation.[318] To that end, he ordered an immediate cessation of all animal fights in Hamburg, threatening violators with arrest. "No longer is the message from the Governor of South Carolina to the Governor of North Carolina to be one of historic conviviality," one newspaper mused. "Now it is, keep your game cocks on your dung hill, and don't send them into my domain to enter the prize ring."[319]

Hamburg also had a reputation as a watering hole wrought with vice and illegalities. It was at a Hamburg saloon where Thomas Butler, one of the ringleaders of the Hamburg Massacre, found himself in a shootout with an Augusta hotel owner.

The town's sullied reputation molded Tillman's desire to impose regulations on alcohol sales. In December 1892, at Tillman's behest, the legislature approved the state's dispensary system, which essentially socialized the sale of alcohol. Tillman reasoned that the dispensary system would also generate more state revenue. "The Dispensary proved to be a practical solution of a vital problem. It was a reasoned compromise between unrestrained drinking and the impracticalities of total Prohibition....So great was his interest in the Dispensary that it became almost an obsession with him."[320]

Adoption of the dispensary came months after Louis Schiller, the Jewish newspaperman who evaded armed vigilantes during the Hamburg Massacre, ran into legal troubles after his election as Hamburg mayor in 1892. Schiller and three others were arrested for selling liquor on Sunday. Schiller and longtime friend Dave Lepfield were each held on $200 bonds. Also arrested, interestingly, was Thomas Butler. The cases were referred to county court, where they were later released.[321]

Hamburg's black market on booze continued. It got to where Tillman recommended re-revoking Hamburg's charter. Schiller protested, saying that revoking the charter would deprive the state of tax revenues and lead to increased lawlessness in Hamburg. "It is claimed by all those with whom the reporter conversed that Hamburg is no more disorderly than any other Carolina town and that violations of the whiskey law no more frequent," the *Chronicle* noted.[322]

Of course, it was difficult for Schiller's protestations to gain any traction, especially since weeks earlier he made the wrong kind of headlines again after shooting at an African American man, maiming the victim's hand. The incident undercut Schiller's position that Hamburg was "no more disorderly" than other South Carolina towns:

> *Hamburg had her usual Sunday shooting scrape. A white man named Lewis* [sic] *Schiller shot at a negro named Gus Preston. The ball went through the negro's hand, inflicting a severe wound.*[323]

Why Schiller shot at the man isn't clear. And while the incident further cast Hamburg in negative light, Tillman ultimately backed off his threat to revoke Hamburg's charter. Instead, he found another way to strip away the floundering town's lingering autonomy. Tillman, who always believed that all local government should fall under state control, got his wish in January 1894 when the legislature approved Act 320, abolishing local and county elections. Local leaders instead were nominated by state lawmakers and appointed by the governor.

Much of Tillman's rationale for Act 320 was meant to block African Americans from holding elected positions of any kind. By stuffing state offices with "Tillmanites," the chances of African Americans landing a political appointment were next to nil.

As it related to Hamburg, stripping loyal governance was yet another nail in the coffin. By 1895, Act 320 became part of the state constitution. Local governments operated under the state's thumb for the next eighty years. It wasn't until 1975, with passage of the Home Rule Act, that greater autonomy returned to local and county governments.[324]

Tillman's caustic nature gained him a populist following, which helped propel him from the governor's mansion to the U.S. Senate. In 1894, Tillman challenged General Butler, who was seeking a fourth term. By now, the career politician was losing his appeal. At one debate in Edgefield, personal attacks flowed freely from the lips of both men. Butler accused Tillman of not paying his newspaper subscription and also "charged Tillman with being a ring and raucous nominee." Tillman replied that Butler lacked courage. "I dare you to give me a primary. You will never do it because you are afraid. Even rings won't save you," Tillman replied.

The debate quickly spiraled out of control, turning into a referendum on Hamburg and drawing the audience into the debate. Factions from each side verbally attacked the other. One Tillman supporter accused Butler of denying his participation in the Hamburg Massacre while in Washington, D.C., but freely taking credit for it back in South Carolina. This attack triggered an immediate response from the Edgefield general. Butler "turned like a panther" and snapped back at the unnamed person. "That is a lie—an infernal lie!" Butler barked.

At this point, a physical confrontation seemed unavoidable among the well-armed crowd. Some rushed the debate stage, exchanging stares and coarse words with one another. Butler and Tillman intervened when a riot appeared imminent. "Nobody knows what prevented the killing and wounding of many men here to-day. For ten minutes men stood with hands on pistols and with knives tightly clutched ready to use those deadly weapons on each other," one newspaper reported.

It didn't take long for the rhetoric to resume. Butler read a certificate signed by eight men stating they never saw Tillman during the Hamburg Massacre. Tillman produced his own certificate, signed by twice as many men, saying he was present—Harrison Butler and Henry Getzen among them. Others in the audience who hadn't signed the certificate proclaimed their support for Tillman. "Yes, you were there!" his backers chanted. "We were with you and saw you!"

Tillman then issued a challenge to anybody skeptical of his participation. "If any man doubts that, let him meet me on the public square," he said.[325] Nobody did. Tillman coasted to victory in November and served continuously in the Senate until his death in on July 3, 1918.

Left: Ben "Pitchfork" Tillman, former South Carolina governor, U.S. senator and participant in the Hamburg Massacre.

Right: General Matthew Calbraith "M.C." Butler. *Courtesy Library of Congress, Prints and Photographs Division, Washington, D.C.*

Then there was the terse yet truculent Henry Getzen, the brother-in-law of Thomas Butler. Curiously, despite having no apparent legal or political experience, Getzen landed Prince Rivers's old job as Hamburg trial justice. In 1878, a brief in the *Edgefield Advertiser* stated that Getzen had set up "a handsome office" in Hamburg.[326] Even more curious, not long after Getzen's appointment, the state legislature in 1880 passed an act restoring Hamburg's charter,[327] which remained in effect well into the twentieth century. Getzen won reelection in 1882 and remained a trial justice until at least 1897, when he doubled as the town's mayor.[328]

Newspapers literally canonized Getzen. In 1897, the *Aiken Times* was "glad to hear Mr. Getzen was not fatally shot and will recover" after one of Getzen's constables accidentally shot him just above the waist while they were apprehending two suspected robbers.

Around the turn of the century, Getzen gained even more prominence when he converted an old mill pond into a popular swimming hole. Getzen's Pond, as the summertime retreat came to be known, became quite the hot spot. Swimmers—many of them naked—turned out in droves to the pond, which today lies feet from the eighteenth fairway at the River Golf Club in modern-day North Augusta. Today, dense forest shields Getzen's Pond from view, but the pond itself remains readably discoverable on most smartphone map apps. "Going there became so popular—for children and adults—that Augusta's J.B. White's advertised free Getzen's swimming passes if you purchased a bathing suit from the store."[329]

When Getzen died in 1920, the Aiken *Journal and Review* lauded the "oriflamme of the Hamburg fight" in a lengthy obituary. "He was then in the prime of youth—manly and brave and handsome. He was always discreet, but feared no one, and whatever appeared to him to be his duty he did it regardless of consequences," the obituary read.[330]

Thomas Butler, however, lived a much different life. Instead of entering politics like others at Hamburg, the son of Robert J. Butler lived like a vagabond, drunk and poor. In 1879, following in his father's footsteps, Butler performed a "demonstration" to showcase his family's "Negro hunting" skills in the unlikeliest of places: New York City. Central Park, to be exact. A troupe performing *Uncle Tom's Cabin* offered him $150 per night for the purpose of using one of his dogs in a scene.[331]

As part of the show, Butler would give a black preacher a head start before turning the dogs loose. The *Edgefield Advertiser* portrayed the show as being all in good fun. "The public must by no means entertain an idea that there is anght [*sic*] of cruelty to either man or beast in this unique entertainment, as the negro in question is devoted to his employer and hounds are well kept for."[332]

Butler made news again in 1893, this time for actions more nefarious than pretending to hunt Black men in the Big Apple. Seventeen years after the Hamburg Massacre, he found himself embroiled in a second Hamburg gunfight, this one originating from a labor dispute. The shootout left a prominent hotel owner dead and injured three others, including Butler.[333]

On the afternoon of May 28, 1893, Butler was lounging in a chair outside Shinall's Saloon, a Hamburg watering hole. A double-barrel shotgun sat beside him, perched upright against the wall. In front of the saloon, a large tree loomed overhead.

Butler would later tell police that he'd only been at the saloon a short time when Joseph Pettyjohn and his family approached in a carriage around 2:00 p.m. and that he only fired at the family in self-defense. He was later charged with murder.[334]

Pettyjohn operated the Arlington Hotel in Augusta and also owned a farm near North Augusta. He was a father of three but had recently lost one of his sons from tuberculosis.[335] Pettyjohn and Butler had been friends, but a week before the shooting they became embroiled in a labor dispute. As newspapers reported, Butler threatened to sue Pettyjohn for poaching one of his employees by the name of Jim Ford. Matters worsened when Butler insulted Pettyjohn's honor, calling him a liar. "Mr. Butler, I will have you arrested for that," Pettyjohn said. "It is not necessary for you to call a man of my age a liar."

"You would not dare to have me arrested sir," Butler replied, wagging his finger at Pettyjohn.

"You hold still and I will show that I will have you arrested," Pettyjohn repeated.

In Butler's version of the story, he claimed that twenty-eight cows pastured at Pettyjohn's farm near North Augusta wandered onto his nearby property at Shultz's Hill, destroying an oat patch. Butler seized the wayward cattle, drove them to one of his pastures and penned them there as collateral until Pettyjohn reimbursed him for his damaged oat patch.

Pettyjohn disputed Butler's account, telling an investigator he received a phone call that the cows were secured in a pen. His family traveled to the field, where they confirmed someone had fenced the cows in a field protected by barbed wire. Pettyjohn contended that this countered Butler's claim the cattle had wandered there. "I came to the conclusion immediately that Tom Butler had them turned out himself," Pettyjohn said. "We looked at the fence and came to the conclusion that the cows had been turned out; that they did not get out on their own hook, but had been turned out."

While there were half-hearted attempts to resolve the dispute amicably, both sides prepared for a bloody outcome. Recalling past difficulties with Butler, Pettyjohn suspected Butler's endgame was extortion. "Some considerable time back Mr. Butler shot one of my cows. I gave $50 for her," Pettyjohn recalled. "I tried to get along with him in peace knowing that he was sort of a ruffian and brow-beat and bull-dozer."[336]

So Pettyjohn, his two sons and five other men armed themselves and departed for North Augusta. If the cows were to be returned, it would be by force. Back in Hamburg, rumors quickly spread that Pettyjohn planned "to kill [Butler] on sight." Fearing the worst, Butler grabbed a shotgun and headed for Shinall's saloon, unaware that Pettyjohn would soon come to him.[337]

As the Pettyjohns approached Butler's oat patch at Shultz's Hill, there was no sign of Butler—only twenty-eight cattle penned in a pasture. So the entourage drove the cows back to Pettyjohn's property and then departed for Augusta.

As Pettyjohn's buggy drove through Hamburg and creaked toward Shinall's saloon, the Pettyjohns spotted Butler lounging on the front porch. Spotting the Pettyjohn buggy at virtually the same time, Butler grabbed his shotgun and opened fire, later saying that the Pettyjohns were "in for a fight."

Pettyjohn said that he was preparing to turn the buggy around when William Pettyjohn, his eldest son, leaped to the ground. Butler sprinted behind the large tree fronting the saloon and kept firing. The rest of the Pettyjohns poured out of the buggy. William sought cover behind a trestle, while his younger brother, Joseph Jr., only fifteen years old at the time, positioned himself thirty to forty yards away, sheltering himself behind the corner of a house. Joseph Sr. fired from the open street, with his wife wailing for everyone to keep firing. Soon the streets of Hamburg sounded like exploding fireworks.

William Pettyjohn took a bullet to the arm during the opening salvo. In the second exchange, he was shot again, this time in the abdomen, while Joseph Sr. suffered a gunshot wound to his foot. In all, about fifteen shots had been fired.

Outnumbered and outgunned, Butler retreated into the saloon to reload. Joseph Sr. pursued, making it within five feet of Butler before the two simultaneously fired at each other. "Pettyjohn received the entire contents of Butler's gun in the stomach," the Aiken newspaper reported. "The deadly stock so [diverted] his aim as to cause Pettyjohn to discharge the full load from one barrel into the ceiling."[338]

Believing that he'd bought time for his escape, Butler darted into a back hallway to reload once again, partially closing the door behind him. Doing so probably saved his life. Joseph Sr., probably running on adrenaline, continued his pursuit and opened fire again when he reached the door. The door deflected the brunt of the Pettyjohn patriarch's assault, although enough buckshot tore through the door, wounding Butler in the face, neck and chest. "Had the door not been closed the discharge would have mortally wounded, if not instantly killed, Butler," the *Courier-Journal* reported.[339]

The carnage would've continued if not for the efforts of William Shinall, owner of the saloon, who ushered Joseph Sr. back outside. Somehow, Joseph Pettyjohn Sr. managed to drive his family back to his Augusta hotel. "Both Mr. Pettyjohn and Will were very weak from loss of blood and when they drove up to the hotel they both had to be assisted to their rooms," the *Edgefield Advertiser* reported. Joseph Pettyjohn Sr. hung on long enough to describe the shooting to a police investigator and newspaper reporter. He died hours later.

William Pettyjohn was seriously hurt, receiving five gunshot wounds—two to the arm, one to the leg and two flesh wounds to the abdomen. Joseph Jr. and Mrs. Pettyjohn were not injured.

Butler received at least twenty-four gunshot wounds to the face, hand, neck and chest. Miraculously, none was considered life-threatening.[340]

After Butler's arrest, his bond was set at $3,000. Defense attorney Daniel Sullivan Henderson, the Aiken attorney who previously represented Butler and others for their participation in the Hamburg Massacre, represented Butler once again. John Gary Evans served as co-counsel.[341]

Following a few postponements, the case was called to trial the week of September 25, 1893. It took the jury only an hour to deliver a not guilty verdict. "There was no doubt after the State's evidence was closed but that Mr. Butler would be acquitted. That was the unanimous opinion," the *Edgefield Advertiser* reported. "No one thought he would be convicted, for the testimony of the prosecution was construed as substantially warranting Mr. Butler to pursue the course he took."[342]

Curiously, none of the South Carolina newspapers covering the case ever mentioned Butler's connection to the Hamburg Massacre. Perhaps it was an oversight. Or perhaps the newspapers did so deliberately to paint him in as positive a light as possible.

Whatever the reason, Butler's final years were uneventful. An obituary published in 1901 for his brother, W.H.H. Butler, stated that Thomas Butler had died three years earlier in his home at the age of forty-three, an inconspicuous end for one of the most cantankerous figures of the Hamburg Massacre.[343]

Chapter 18

Fires, Floods and Disease

As America entered the twentieth century, innovation and opportunity abounded in a rapidly expanding community called North Augusta. Situated north of Hamburg, North Augusta's roots date to 1889, when James U. Jackson, an Augusta developer, established the North Augusta Land Company.

Within two years, Jackson had built the Thirteenth Street Bridge upriver from Hamburg, providing an alternative link between North Augusta and Augusta. Electricity and a trolley line came by 1897, providing much-needed infrastructure.

In 1903, the Hampton Terrace Hotel opened. Situated atop a large hill overlooking Hamburg and Augusta, the Hampton Terrace embodied the opulence from the period, boasting five floors and three hundred rooms. Amenities included tennis courts, riding stables and an eighteen-hole golf course. John D. Rockefeller, Harvey Firestone and William Howard Taft all stayed at the hotel.[344]

Three years later, the Hampton Terrace served as host site for a banquet fêting supporters of a major North Augusta incorporation vote. In April 1906, a ballot question establishing the town passed handily by a three-to-one margin. A crowd of one hundred people attended the banquet, which Jackson himself organized. "There will be a meeting of the officers of the village in a few days, and the laws to govern the new municipality will be made up. The police and fire departments will be looked after and a number of other improvements inaugurated."[345]

North Augusta prospered. Yet barely a mile from the lush fairways and glitzy hotel ballrooms, a series of fires, floods and disease squeezed the remaining life from the struggling town of Hamburg.

On the morning of May 9, 1891, a massive fire consumed numerous buildings in Hamburg. That spring had been unusually dry, with only two inches of rain falling in all of April, half the historical norm.[346] May was even more arid, the last measurable rain having not fallen since April 23. Farmers suffered. "Cool nights have slightly damaged the cotton crop, and the absence of rain makes the present outlook very unfavorable east of the lower Mississippi," one report noted.[347] All that was needed for a major fire was a spark, and that spark was lurking around the corner.

In 1891, the Richmond and Danfield Railroad Company operated three daily routes servicing Augusta, Georgia. Two arrived in Augusta at 8:15 a.m. and 10:15 a.m.; a third departed at 10:45 a.m. All three passed through Hamburg.[348] On May 9, as one of these trains chugged into town, a spark flew from the track. It landed on the roof of a stable; the dry shingle roof caught fire and quickly spread. By the time the blaze was discovered, it was too late. The barn burned to the ground, killing a horse. It also burned a train trestle before spreading to a home situated above a store. "[The fire] crept along the fences and outhouses until the brick residence was reached and in quick order the entire place was enveloped in flames," the *Yorkville Enquirer* reported.[349]

The inferno continued spreading, engulfing more homes and businesses. Looters swept in, stealing anything of value. Hamburg was virtually left in ruin. "The fire has about swept Hamburg away, all the business centre now being gone."[350]

With no real infrastructure or basic services, Hamburg had also become unsafe. Few dared to travel through town without first arming themselves. "Now it is nothing but almost a howling wilderness. Hamburg is surely an evidence of what narrow-minded illiberal citizens can do. It now serves but one purpose. It is the battle-ground for game cocks and bull dogs," one report said.[351] "Instead of being the pride, Hamburg has become an eye-sore to the state, and the advice has been given out that her last day shall not be far distant," another account stated.[352]

In 1895, the R.J. Rutherford Brick Company briefly did business in the floundering town. A pair of Rutherford buildings exists today at the mouth of the River North subdivision. But business was brief, as floods continued to pummel the unprotected town.

The remnants of a building formerly part of W.J. Rutherford & Company Brickyard in Hamburg at the entrance to the River North subdivision. *Courtesy the author.*

In September 1908, a massive headline screamed the following:[353]

Terrible Havoc Feared from Floods
Upper Carolina Was Deluged Tuesday
RAINFALL TUESDAY NIGHT WAS TERRIFIC

In Hamburg, the town literally smelled like death after the 1908 flood. The odor of human corpses and dead livestock hovered over the Savannah River like a toxic fog. Newspapers noted that the noxious odor of untreated sewage made the air virtually unbreathable. "A fearful stench covers the flood area like a pall. Odor of decayed vegetable and animal matter, the vile smell of unflushed sewers, the smell of filthy mud that in places lies piled in great heaps waist high—these and a dozen odors are everywhere."

The foul stench lingered for days. "Inside doors it is oppressive, outside it is worse," the report continued. "When one leaves the city behind he leaves its stench behind but not until then."[354]

The flood of 1908 wasn't the first or the last to inundate Hamburg and the surrounding area. It was, though, a statewide event, with reports of major damage or deaths spanning from Aiken to Charleston. In Anderson, about ninety-five miles north of Hamburg, twelve inches of rain fell during a twenty-four-hour period.[355]

Making matters worse, a dam seven miles north of Hamburg burst, channeling water previously diverted to the Augusta Canal farther down the Savannah River instead, adding more misery. "The great flood of water found its way into the city and that night, from 15th street to the eastern boundary, Augusta was under from six to twelve feet of water, which is gradually rising," the *Fort Mill Times* reported.[356]

The *Watchman and Southron* (Sumter) reported that the Savannah River rose three feet per hour for several hours. "The gauge reading on the Savannah River was the highest this afternoon ever known."[357]

Upstate, the downpours were described as a "rain blizzard" in Greenville. Spartanburg County saw the heaviest rain in its history since 1846. One-fourth to half of the county's cotton crop was lost.[358]

Casualty reports varied greatly. In his book *Yesterday's Augusta*, author Arthur Ray Rowland pegged the death toll at eighteen. A 1908 newspaper report, however, stated at least twenty-two people died. The same report went on to say a steamer captain observed at least twenty-five bodies.[359]

Another news report claimed that at least sixty people died, with African American laborers accounting for most of the deaths. Two women drowned in plain view when floodwaters caused their buggy to overturn.[360]

The flood severed railroad, telephone and telegraph services. One report noted, "The Savannah River has been rushing down Broad Street in a muddy torrent breast deep."[361]

Seeking higher ground proved just as lethal, as explosions rocked several warehouses storing quantities of lime. Certain lime compounds, such as calcium oxide, can contribute to explosions when exposed to high quantities of water. The lime itself isn't combustible, but it can give off gas and fumes that are explosive when coming into contact with other substances.[362] This apparently happened at the Nixon Grocery warehouse in Augusta as the 1908 flood raged, according to one report.

> *Apparently safe from the engulfing flood, the helpless refugees were struck dumb with a new horror a moment later when flames burst from the warehouse on all sides caused by the slacking lime. Choosing death in the flood to cremation in the flames, the men began jumping into one of the swiftest currents that raged through the terror stricken city. A current that is spoken of today as "running a mile a minute" swept them to instant death.*

One of those leaping was Harry Carr, a prominent businessman. His brother, C.D. Carr, recalled how he watched in horror as his sibling jumped to his death:

> *I knew Harry could not swim, and when I saw him jump I closed my eyes on one of the greatest tragedies of my life. I knew he was gone beyond all earthly help. The muddy waters were painted hideously blood red in the light of the awful flames. The current was roaring like thunder and nothing on this earth could live in its mighty grasp.*[363]

Similar fires broke out throughout Aiken County. One inferno burned a warehouse in North Augusta. Another destroyed a train of forty cars in Hamburg. A third fire consumed a train with fourteen boxcars, including one filled with goats. All perished. An even more grisly scene unfolded in the Savannah River, where "scores of horses, mules and other stock, could be seen among the debris floating the river."[364]

For centuries, flooding had ravaged the Savannah River region. The first recorded instance occurred in 1741. By the 1750s, some locals claimed that the river overflowed "once or twice a year."[365]

On January 16, 1796, a Saturday, the river "rose to an alarming height," and within a few hours, most of Augusta was submerged under four to five inches of water. Floodwaters steadily rose until Sunday morning, when the depths reached two feet in some locations. Aside from a few homes on high ground, the entire town was under water. At its peak, the river rose an estimated thirty-five feet above its normal height. Many cattle drowned, and tobacco fields were left in ruin. "It is certain, however, that the memory of the oldest inhabitant recollects nothing like this inundation, nor, may it be justly precedent supposed, was it ever before at so prodigious a height."

During the 1796 flood, a man marooned on a raft in the raging river saved himself by leaping to a nearby bridge moments before the vessel crashed into the structure. The force of impact was so great that parts of the bridge crumbled into raging river, although enough of it remained for the man to land safely. The raftsman "cleared himself with successful speed and an astonishing presence of mind from the dreadful crash of the last fragment of this once great and useful communication between Georgia and South Carolina."[366]

Similarly destructive flooding struck at least once every decade.[367] Flooding in the middle part of the nineteenth century greatly contributed to Hamburg's first downfall before the Civil War. "While the town rebuilt after each one, the effort began to sap the community's economic vitality."[368]

Augusta suffered as well. A flood in 1888 prompted city leaders there to finally begin discussing flood control, although nothing substantive emerged beyond the discussion phase. It wasn't until the 1908 flood that proposed levee improvements finally came before voters, although the referendum failed. Subsequent floods in 1912 and 1913 finally moved the needle forward on flood prevention, although Hamburg was left out of the discussion.

A 2002 North Augusta study attributed Hamburg's flood-prone nature to three springs located south of the town's corporate limits that hindered "drainage." Poor soil compounded the problem.[369] "Hamburg reveals almost exclusively poorly drained Chewacla soils—consistent with the descriptions of the site as 'swampy,' and helping to explain the need for a ditch running down the middle of the one [of] the village's main east-west streets," the study stated.[370]

As if fires and floods weren't enough, disease plagued Hamburg's remaining residents. In June 1899, an outbreak of smallpox swept through the town. Aiken County residents mostly feared unsubstantiated claims that the disease was being spread by "vagabond negroes" who were "roaming all about the country."

Judge Henry Getzen of Hamburg Massacre infamy appealed to the governor's office for help. Augusta took in some of the invalids, although the city's resources were already stretched thin, owing to a massive downtown fire.[371]

By the 1920s, Hamburg was more of a settlement than an actual municipality. The streets were gone. There was essentially no functioning government. Aside from a few shacks, what buildings remained were virtual ruins. "Hamburg strikingly illustrates the fate that can befall any town or city. One passes through Hamburg now on the Southern way to Augusta, but unless it were called to one's attention it would probably not be known when the town is passed."[372]

In the surrounding region, progress had finally been made to combat the floods that had inundated neighboring communities for more than a century. In 1915, following a multitude of major floods, construction of a new levee raised hopes that disastrous flooding could be contained. It cost about $3 million (about $75 million in 2019 dollars) to build the new levee at the head gates of the Augusta Canal to Butler Creek. In 1928, the levee was strengthened and lengthened.[373]

These improvements, however, came too late to save Hamburg, as a pair of floods on the eve of the Great Depression dealt the final blow. The first of these flood events struck in 1928. In August of that year, a Category 2 hurricane slammed the Caribbean and Florida peninsula. Later named the Fort Pierce Hurricane of 1928, the storm weakened into a tropical depression by the time it reached South Carolina, although it still spawned three tornadoes and caused torrential downpours. Caesar's Head in Greenville County reported eleven inches of rain in twenty-four hours.[374]

In Hamburg and Augusta, the Savannah River reached a record height of forty feet, five inches, remaining at that level for three hours. Rain fell at a rate of four inches per hour at the North Augusta bridge. Unsurprisingly, Hamburg suffered the most:

> *The flood waters of the stream continue to hold in North Augusta and Hamburg, covering the trolley tracks and highway in the North Augusta section, while inhabitants of a negro settlement in Hamburg are still without shelter, due to the waters having flooded their homes. Manufacturing plants in those two sections also remain waterbound. It will probably be a full day or more before all the water recedes in those sections.*[375]

Another flood the following year was even worse. Two rainstorms, punctuated by another hurricane, dumped more than two feet of rain in seven days. From September 26 to September 28, more than nine inches of rain drowned Hamburg. Nearly seven inches fell on September 27 alone.[376]

The Savannah River was already within inches of spilling over the Fifth Street Bridge. A person sitting on the bridge could've dipped their toes in the swelling river.[377] So when the Great Bahamas Hurricane of 1929 arrived, the soil and rock levee built in 1915 failed. Hamburg didn't stand a chance.

Ironically, it was a slow hurricane season in 1929. Only five tropical systems formed, three of them hurricanes, in the Atlantic Ocean. One storm was classified as major (winds of 110 miles per hour or greater).[378] It was this storm, the Great Bahamas Hurricane, that forced out the remaining Hamburg residents.

The 1929 hurricane crossed the Florida peninsula into the Gulf of Mexico before turning due north and then northeast, passing directly over Hamburg.[379] It had already devastated the Bahamas with 125-mile-per-hour winds, slamming into central Nassau on September 26 as a Category 4 hurricane. Some sources claimed that winds reached 155 miles per hour. The storm remained a major hurricane as it barreled west, crossing the Florida Keys with sustained winds of 115 miles per hour.

The hurricane eventually weakened into a tropical storm before making a third landfall near Apalachicola, Florida. By October, it swirled in the skies above Hamburg.[380]

Ten inches of rain fell October 1–2, and more than seventeen had fallen since September 26, an astonishingly high average of nearly 2.5 inches per day for seven consecutive days. Levee or no levee, nothing could stop the flooding. Hamburg was doomed. The 1929 freshet was the flood of the millennium:[381]

> *The "Main Street" of Hamburg was itself a swirling river bed and the waters lapped about the tops of the chimneys and pounded against the shingles of the roofs. In some of the houses left standing one can see household furnishings stuffed into the attic, or on the second floor piled upon tables. This bears mute testimony to the hope of Hamburg dwellers that the flood would not reach them there. But it did. In most instances the muddy waters went clear to the roofs, the silt and slime upon the shingles revealing the high mark of the overflow.*[382]

At least a dozen houses were entirely swept away and are lost somewhere in the swamps below Augusta. An equal number of residences were left twisted and torn, some of them being moved a block away and leaning against trees.

Flood victims faced disease as well. Stagnating water turned Hamburg into a mosquito-breeding hotbed, with nearly 120 cases of malaria reported. To eradicate mosquito egg infestations, American Red Cross relief workers pumped three hundred gallons of kerosene and crude oil in hard-to-drain areas.

Typhoid fever was another problem. Virtually every water source—springs, wells, pumps or any other water supply—became contaminated by floodwater and sewage. Potable water didn't exist anywhere. Health officials warned residents to avoid drinking water at all costs without first boiling it.[383]

The Red Cross reported that thirty-seven homes and fourteen barns were destroyed. Another forty-one homes and fourteen barns suffered damage. Ninety-five families lost home furnishings. Large quantities of livestock and poultry were also lost. "Hamburg's gone now," one resident lamented.

The Red Cross assisted roughly seventy families. Help came in the form of clothing, furnishings and livestock. An estimated $10,350 in aid (about $151,000 in 2019 dollars) was provided.[384] Aid, however, came at a cost. Anyone seeking assistance had to move. The Red Cross insisted that anyone choosing to remain in Hamburg would not qualify for assistance. There were no exceptions. "Under no circumstances will aid be extended to families who remain in Hamburg. In offering assistance in this work, the American Red Cross feels that it will discharge its obligation in Hamburg as a relief agency at no time in the future will it expect to be called upon to render aid there."[385]

Help came in the form of building assistance, food, clothing and household furnishings.[386] In some cases, the Red Cross purchased entire lots a few miles away, not only to prevent rebuilding in Hamburg but also to subsidize the relocation of Hamburg residents to higher ground. "The Red Cross intends to clear out Hamburg so that it will not be responsible for any future disasters there."[387]

Interestingly, to this day the Red Cross still owns a parcel in what used to be Hamburg.[388] A Red Cross official with knowledge of the property and its future plans could not be reached.

While providing tangible relief, nothing the Red Cross provided could preserve Hamburg itself. "If Henry Shultz [*sic*] ghost stalks about those ruins it must be an apparition that bears a great sorrow. Sherman did not know half as much about destroying towns as does the Savannah River when it goes on a rampage."[389]

Chapter 19

The Meriwether Monument

As Hamburg stood on the cusp of dissolution, the handful of remaining residents must've looked up toward North Augusta in disgust.

On February 16, 1916, the addition of a new monument in Calhoun Square would shape racial debate for decades. It was in this spot where hundreds of North Augustans assembled around the newly christened Meriwether Monument to commemorate Thomas McKie Meriwether, the lone white person killed during the Hamburg Massacre.[390]

Forged from Winnsboro granite, the Meriwether Monument stands twenty-one feet tall and weighs twenty-seven thousand pounds. It was jointly funded by the McKie Meriwether Monument Association and South Carolina General Assembly, the latter body kicking in $400.

Inscribed around the monument's base is a passage as divisive today as it was more than a century ago:

> *In Memory of Thomas McKie Meriwether Who on 8th July 1876, gave his life that the civilization builded by his fathers might be preserved for their children's unimpaired.*
>
> *In youths glad morning the unfinished years of manhood stretching before him, with clear knowledge and courageous willingness, he accepted death and found forever the grateful remembrance of all who know high and generous service in the maintaining of those civic and social institutions which the men and women of his race had struggled through the centuries to establish in South Carolina. What more can a man do than to lay down his life.*

Erected in 1916, the Meriwether Monument uses racially derisive language to honor the lone white man killed during the Hamburg Massacre while failing to mention the seven African Americans who were executed. *Courtesy the author.*

> *In life he exemplified the highest ideal of Anglo-Saxon Civilization. By his death he assured to the children of his beloved land the supremacy of that idea. As the flame of life was quenched, it lit the blaze of victory.*
>
> *This memorial is erected to the young hero of the Hamburg Riot, by the state, under an act of the general assembly, with the aid of admiring friends.*[391]

Efforts to build the monument can be traced to January 1914. An op-ed published in *The State* (Columbia) newspaper called on state lawmakers to commemorate Meriwether with a memorial. To whites, Meriwether died a martyr while defending the "white cause":

> *The main object in my writing this sketch of McKie Meriwether, in which I have had to narrate in my humble and feeble way the events that caused him to give his blood for his country's good, is to stir up some recognition on the part of our legislature to him and his illustrious memory to which I*

> *look with pride and reverence....Monuments have so rarely in the history of our country been erected to people in the ordinary private stations of life that we think it time to make an exception to the rule and give T. McKie Meriwether some memorial recognition of his valor and heroism by placing a monument over his resting place.*[392]

Two years later, the unveiling of "the handsome monument," as the *Edgefield Advertiser* coined it, turned into a spectacle. Singers in the North Augusta High School girls' chorus gave an "inspiring" and "patriotic" performance complemented by the school's orchestra. Democratic politicians past and present lauded Meriwether in a series of longwinded speeches. "In the town of North Augusta, in the centre of Calhoun square [*sic*], stands a massive granite shaft that will be a silent tribute for many generations to come to the brave and patriotic young man, McKie Meriwether, whose life was immolated on his country's altar in July 1876," the *Edgefield Advertiser* reported.

VIPs on hand lumped gushing praise on young Meriwether, extolling his valor while simultaneously castigating African Americans and Republican sympathizers as corrupt and oppressive. Among those speaking was Daniel Sullivan Henderson, the Aiken defense attorney who represented the sixty men charged, but never tried, for their roles in the Hamburg Massacre. Like other Hamburg Massacre alumni, Henderson parlayed his association to the events of 1876 into a successful political career, serving in the state Senate. "McKie Meriwether perished for the cause of liberty and we are here today to perpetuate his memory and the cause which he represented," Henderson said. "As his flame of life was quenched, he lit the flame of victory for the white people of South Carolina."[393]

In his fifteen-page address, Henderson left no ambiguity that the driving force behind the Meriwether Monument was to reaffirm Black suppression. He specifically noted that the monument "redeemed the Palmetto State from the yoke of the African and the stranger, and which established beyond question that this is a white man's country, to be ruled by white man forever."

Henderson went on to hail Meriwether as a "hero for white independence," likening him to Leonidas I, the Spartan king who battled invading Persians at Thermopylae in 480 BC. He denied hating African Americans, portraying them instead as pawns of Radical Republican oppression of southerners. "No white man's property or liberty was safe, except what his own strong arm protected," he said. "Ignorant judges sat on the bench. The Supreme Court became composed of a superannuated Jew, a shrewd carpet-bagger and an ignorant black negro."[394]

Henderson went on to label the state's Black residents as pitiable and ignorant, proclaiming "social equality will never be tolerated" in the South. "We have lived to see the day when the negro, ceasing to be in position to act as a tool for political charlatans, is satisfied with his normal condition, as an equal of the white man in the eye of the law, but not his equal politically or socially."[395]

Piling on was Representative J.P. DeLaughter, the state lawmaker who lobbied for the monument, speaking in "picturesque terms" of his support of Meriwether. DeLaughter is credited with rallying the legislature to override a gubernatorial veto so the monument would be funded. "The battle of Hamburg was not a massacre. It was a rebellion against wrong, a blow for the right, an armed rebuke," DeLaughter proclaimed.[396]

Of course, DeLaughter's recollection of the Hamburg Massacre was an exaggeration at best. DeLaughter claimed that Meriwether "snatched a rifle from the hands of his aged father" and that he rushed into the thick of the fighting at Hamburg and "died for his State and white supremacy," when in reality Meriwether and his father merely exchanged weapons. The bullet that killed young Meriwether took him out long before the "thick of the fighting."[397]

In the years that followed the dedication, the buzz over the Meriwether Monument quietly faded, essentially becoming a political and social speakeasy. In 1922, the same man who penned an op-ed calling for a monument penned another opinion piece describing Meriwether as "chivalrous" and the "very flower of the young men" of Aiken and Edgefield Counties. A pair of news reports in the 1950s and 1960s anecdotally referred to Meriwether's actions in the Hamburg Massacre but stayed silent on the monument.[398]

Efforts to address the Hamburg Massacre never began in earnest until 2004, when a plaque telling the basic story of the massacre went up near the Hamburg town limits. Sadly, the memorial fell victim to vandals and thieves.[399]

It wasn't until 2008 that local media started openly questioning the Meriwether Monument. An in-depth report dubbed "Monumental Injustice" recounted the events of the Hamburg Massacre and local historian efforts to establish a park commemorating Hamburg. A companion editorial openly called for the monument—or the inscription, at least—to be removed. "What would today be called a hate crime was then seen as an act to put black people in their place and restore white dominance to Southern society. It is appalling that such an outrageous event is still honored with a place of distinction in a North Augusta city park," the editorial read. "North Augusta leaders should remove the historically inaccurate plaques that were placed to honor such overt racism."[400]

Nothing substantive occurred however. In 2009, the City of North Augusta acquired three parcels in the vicinity of Hamburg, paying $175,700 for the land, raising hopes that it could be repurposed into previously envisioned historic park. A newspaper editorial noted the primary goal was to beautify the Jefferson Davis Highway corridor. "That area was also of interest to a variety of North Augustans concerned with the preservation of the history of the area, since the land around that area was once Hamburg, one of the townships that precedes North Augusta in history....The purchase will give City officials some control over what happens next."[401]

In the years that have passed, the land has remained dormant. No parks were ever built. No tributes to Hamburg took shape. North Augusta taxpayers are still waiting for what happens next after the nearly $176,000 investment.

Mayor Bob Pettit peripherally addressed the properties at a recent community meeting in Carrsville, where the remaining Hamburg residents relocated after the 1929 flood. Pettit was noncommittal about repurposing the former Hamburg tracts, saying that he didn't know about the properties and was still looking into them. There have been no further updates regarding the property since the meeting.[402]

Pettit went on to say that a previous mayor once floated grandiose plans to build large hotels along the riverfront where Hamburg used to exist. A local pastor spoke with dismay over how those plans would drive up property values, thereby driving up taxes and making Carrsville an unaffordable place to live. Gentrification would likely follow.[403]

The affluent River Club community, where home values range between $600,000 and $1.6 million, according to Aiken County property records, has also expressed reticence over development bordering its neighborhood. In June 2007, some homeowners went into a tizzy over a rezoning request that might connect it to Sand Pit Road, which also borders the remnants of Hamburg.

Residents feared that the rezoning would potentially link the upscale neighborhood, which ends in a cul de sac, with Jefferson Davis Highway, raising traffic and "security concerns." They backed off after city leaders assured them the River Club would be left intact. "Our position was that the rezoning doesn't change anybody's rights that existed prior to the rezoning, and the City is not doing anything to widen the road or cut a road," said Lark Jones, the town's former mayor.[404]

The Society Building in Carrsville is an original Hamburg structure that was moved inland after the flood of 1929. *Courtesy the author.*

The North Augusta Heritage Council eventually created a historical marker calling attention to the events of the Hamburg Massacre, but the marker didn't name any of the participants. Fearing theft and vandalism, its creators kept the marker safely locked away in a local church. It wasn't until March 6, 2016, not long after the 100th anniversary of the Meriwether Monument christening, that the historical marker was placed at the Society Building, an original Hamburg structure that had been relocated to Carrsville along with the remaining residents of Hamburg. A second marker naming all eight who died during the Hamburg Massacre was placed into the ground.

"As a gesture of good will," Thomas McKie Meriwether's name was also etched on the plaque, sandwiched between Jim Cook, the town sheriff slain in the street in gruesome fashion, and Alfred Myniart, one of the African Americans executed later that night.[405]

In 2018, North Augusta City Council adopted a resolution condemning the Meriwether Monument. The resolution also created the Calhoun Park Committee, which was charged with developing a solution to the Meriwether Monument. It took the committee two years to present its recommendations, the work slowed in part to the COVID-19 pandemic and also disagreements over the initial draft plan.

A marker in Carrsville names all eight who died during the Hamburg Massacre. *Courtesy the author.*

Initially, the group proposed adding a separate memorial to the Meriwether Monument calling attention to the African Americans who died. Pettit also suggested moving existing Hamburg markers in Carrsville to Calhoun Park. At some point, additional but unspecified markers and/or monuments telling Carrsville's history would replace the markers moved to Calhoun Park. The reasoning given was that the Carrsville markers could be moved relatively quickly. Reaction in Carrsville was predictably and overwhelmingly negative. "You can leave holes to move that new monument, but the hole that you leave in the spirit of North Augusta is going to be a hole that none of you will ever be able to repair. I don't care what you put in its place," one resident noted.[406]

Also affecting matters is the South Carolina Heritage Act. Adopted in 2000, the act protects most historical monuments and memorials:

> *No Revolutionary War, War of 1812, Mexican War, War Between the States, Spanish-American War, World War I, World War II, Korean War, Vietnam War, Persian Gulf War, Native American, or African-American History monuments or memorials erected on public property of the State or any of its political subdivisions may be relocated, removed,*

> *disturbed, or altered. No street, bridge, structure, park, preserve, reserve, or other public area of the State or any of its political subdivisions dedicated in memory of or named for any historic figure or historic event may be renamed or rededicated. No person may prevent the public body responsible for the monument or memorial from taking proper measures and exercising proper means for the protection, preservation, and care of these monuments, memorials, or nameplates.*

A two-thirds vote in both chambers is required to overrule this requirement, a virtual impossibility in deeply red South Carolina. It's been accomplished only once—after a white supremacist gunned down nine Black parishioners in a Charleston church. In response to the Charleston shooting, at 1:10 a.m. on July 9, 2015, the South Carolina General Assembly adopted Act 80, which ordered the removal of the Confederate Battle Flag from statehouse grounds. Even then, it took thirteen hours of exhaustive debate before House members ultimately voted 94–20 (78.7 percent), hardly an overwhelming vote. It was adopted on July 14, 2015.[407]

Chapter 20

Marching Past the Massacre

With each step they took toward the Meriwether Monument, the chorus of protestor chants grew steadily louder.

"Black Lives Matter!"

"Let me breathe!"

"Take it down!"

On June 20, 2020, under a blazing hot sun, a procession of two hundred people, most of them forty years old or younger, slowly marched in protest toward the Meriwether Monument. Many wore masks, a sign of the times during the COVID-19 pandemic. Others hoisted signs bearing such messages as "No Justice, No Peace," "End White Silence" and "Silence Supports Violence" as they scaled North Augusta's Georgia Avenue toward Calhoun Park, where the monument resides.

As the North Augusta protestors rendezvoused at the entrance to Calhoun Park, hip hop music booming from a pair of speakers greeted them. It was a stark contrast to the North Augusta High School choir and orchestra that serenaded a white supremacist more than a century earlier.

Groups of strategically placed police officers stood on nearby hills, overlooking the protests. There were no arrests, no riots and no vandalism—only inspirational speeches and calls for politicians to act. Unify North Augusta, an independent organization aligned but not affiliated with Black Lives Matter, put together the two-hour protest. "We will no longer tolerate systematic oppression and racism in America," Unify North Augusta organizer Brandy Mitchell declared through a megaphone. "We stand here

About two hundred protestors march up Georgia Avenue in North Augusta in June 2020 to protest the Meriwether Monument. *Courtesy the author.*

in North Augusta next to this monument that says we are less than…that only the Anglo-Saxon race matters. It has no place in our community and we want that monument down."[408]

While the rally called greater attention to the Meriwether Monument's tainted past, it didn't sway local and state leaders, who were conspicuously absent from the June 20 protest.

Weeks after the protest, the South Carolina Attorney General's Office issued a scathing indictment of the Meriwether Monument, declaring that it isn't protected by the South Carolina Heritage Act but also stopping short of authorizing local leaders to remove it. "The Meriwether Monument, in our view, is offensive for what it stands for—White Supremacy….We cannot imagine that the General Assembly intended the Heritage Act to protect such an obviously hateful testament to the racial practices of the past as this Monument is."

The opinion specifically goes on to state that the responsibility of removing the monument falls to the General Assembly, not local government, because the General Assembly adopted legislation to place the monument in North Augusta. "It is our advice that North Augusta proceed directly to the General Assembly for relief from the offensive

A group of Unify North Augusta protestors surround the Meriwether Monument during a protest in June 2020. *Courtesy the author.*

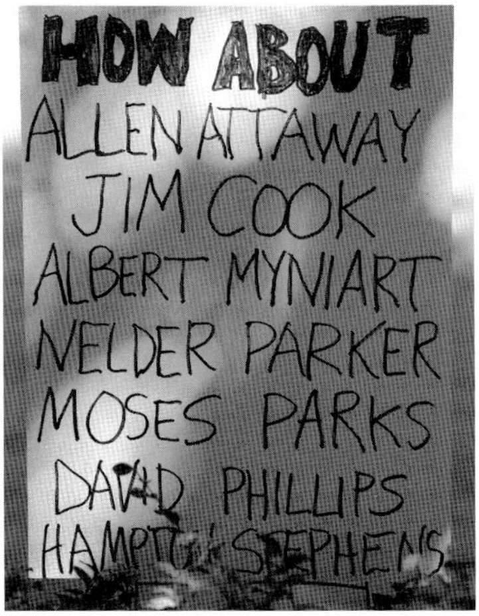

A sign bearing the names of the seven African Americans killed during the Hamburg Massacre. *Courtesy the author.*

nature of this Monument. This Office supports and would applaud the General Assembly's repeal of these statutes erecting the Meriwether Monument."[409]

The General Assembly isn't likely to act anytime soon though. Representative Bill Taylor (R-Aiken) said that he planned to introduce a budget proviso that would penalize cities and counties that remove monuments by withholding a portion of state funding. He called the attorney general opinion "inartfully written," saying that it doesn't provide a definitive answer on whether North Augusta can remove the Meriwether Monument. "The Heritage Act has no teeth. There's no real punishment for violating the Heritage Act," Taylor said. "You have to turn it upside down and hold it up to the light to figure it out."[410]

Senate Majority Leader Shane Massey (R-Edgefield) doesn't support removing monuments either. His comments came in the context of a separate effort to remove a statue of Ben Tillman from statehouse grounds. "I wouldn't support it. I think Ben Tillman was one of the most evil S.O.B.'s that ever lived. It's a reminder of where this state has been, and part of my charge is to make sure that we don't go back there."[411]

Others, like Senator Tom Young (R-Aiken), say that they are open taking action as long as it's in accordance with the city's wishes. "We are waiting to hear from the city and I plan to be attentive to what the local officials want," Young said. "I support telling the full Hamburg story including remembering the others killed."[412]

For now, support for the Meriwether Monument continues to rely on misinformation, false narratives and outright fiction. On June 15, 2020, at a council meeting prior to a vote on issuing a protest permit, some speakers saw no problem with the monument. In a stunning display, one man erroneously claimed that Thomas McKie Meriwether fought alongside the African Americans during the Hamburg Massacre. "I went up to the monument today and read what it said. I saw nothing white supremacist about it. If I'm not mistaken, wasn't Mr. Meriwether killed by white Democrats while fighting with the Black militia? I believe he was.

And if we tear down this monument, then I think we need to go over into Carrsville and tear down that monument that's dedicated to the Blacks, the Black militia," the man said.[413]

Another pro-monument speaker claimed that the phrase "highest ideal of Anglo-Saxon civilization" etched in the inscription was not racist. He thought it represented religious inclusiveness instead. "The Anglo-Saxon heritage happens to be a religious heritage. When I read the religious text of the Anglo-Saxon people, in there I learned one God created one man and one woman. I think it's a mighty supreme idea that we're one family," the man said.[414]

Of course these viewpoints ignore the words young Meriwether himself uttered in 1876, moments before his death (emphasis added): "*We're going to kill every God damned nigger that there was in Hamburg, and then I'm going to try the women and children.*" They also ignore the white supremacist proclamations that state politicians gave during the Meriwether Monument dedication in 1916. The monument "redeemed the Palmetto State from the yoke of the African and the stranger, and which established beyond question that this is a white man's country, to be ruled by white man forever," former state Senator Daniel Sullivan Henderson pledged.

Confederate monuments have been toppling left and right in the wake of George Floyd, Rayshard Brooks and other Black Americans who've died at the hands of police brutality. Memorials honoring antebellum and Confederate-era figures have come down in Dallas, New Orleans and other major cities. Here in the Palmetto State, the Charleston City Council (SC) voted to remove a statue of John C. Calhoun, a former vice president, notorious white supremacist and ardent supporter of slavery.[415]

North Augusta has been slow to follow suit, ostensibly choosing to leave the Meriwether Monument firmly entrenched in the city's center. In November 2018, council members did approve a resolution denouncing the monument. It also created the Calhoun Park Committee, tasking the panel to investigate ways to address the monument and present a formal report with recommendations to city council.[416] That report, presented in August 2020, was similar to the proposal unveiled during the February 2019 community meeting. It proposed adding to the existing monument display in two phases.

Phase 1 calls for positioning three "interpretive panels" at a cost of $8,000 to $10,000 to provide historical context to the Hamburg Massacre and why the monument was erected in 1916. Phase 2 proposed adding a sculpture themed in unity and diversity at a cost of about $200,000, with public and private funds covering the cost.

Council members accepted the report as information but took no action. To the council's credit, members chose to discuss the attorney general's opinion publicly instead of retreating into executive session. They directed Kelly Zier, the city attorney, to seek a definitive answer from the South Carolina General Assembly on who actually owns the monument. The underlying desire was to avoid litigation from a third party, which Zier said was a distinct possibility should the city act unilaterally.[417]

The Meriwether Monument pays homage to a man who never lived in Aiken County, let alone North Augusta. Meriwether was born in Edgefield County in 1852 and is buried in McCormick County. His only tie to Hamburg was trying to kill its Black citizens and getting killed in the process. Hardly an honorable legacy.

The lethargic process of addressing the Meriwether Monument is curious given that the monument has stood for more than a century, and after nearly two years of meetings, little progress has been made. The writing has been on the wall—in the case of the Meriwether Monument, on the obelisk—for more than a century.

Although many denounce the Meriwether Monument as a racist relic, unrepresentative of civilized society, few agree on what its future should be: "Move the monument." "Remove and rewrite the monument's inscription." "Add markers to the monument." "Build a separate monument elsewhere." "Leave the monument alone." Local and state leaders continue to play hot potato with this grab bag of ideas, although nothing has caught fire.

Although it comes as small consolation to Hamburg's ancestors, the City of North Augusta has preserved Hamburg's legacy in one important way: by successfully competing economically with Augusta. John Hammond and Henry Shultz would be proud of how the North Augusta riverfront has transformed in recent years.

The semi-private River Golf Club, which opened in 1998, lures South Carolina and Georgia golfers. Nearby, million-dollar homes line the Savannah River in the River Club and River North subdivision. A pair of vintage Hamburg structures remains near the latter neighborhood's entrance. All this prime real estate occupies property that used to make up Hamburg.

In 2006, high-end homes and trendy restaurants sprang up in the upscale Hammond's Ferry community on the site of what was once Campbellton. A segment of the North Augusta Greeneway bicycle and walking trail meanders through it. Riverside Village, North Augusta's newest development, lies between Hammond's Ferry and the River Club.

The Meriwether Monument serves as the centerpiece of the meticulously manicured grounds of Calhoun Park in North Augusta. *Courtesy the author.*

A hotel, upscale apartments and a baseball stadium draw more visitors. In Henry Shultz–like fashion, the City of North Augusta used generous tax breaks to lure the Augusta GreenJackets minor-league baseball team from Augusta to North Augusta.[418]

Construction continues on a $2.6 million amphitheater. Included in that figure is $100,000 for a posh water fountain characterized as a "mini-Bellagio," referring to the famous Las Vegas hotel with lavish water displays.[419]

Meanwhile, Hamburg remains frozen in time, its remnants succumbing to neglect. It's a tragic fate considering Hamburg is where wagons once lined up outside town to trade, where riverboats ran regularly to and from Charleston and where the Charleston and Hamburg Railroad once ended. Now only ruins remain—ruins that stand in stark contrast to the lush landscaping and manicured gardens surrounding the Meriwether Monument two miles away.

Therein lies the sad irony. As new golf courses, baseball stadiums and high-end housing spring up, the last of the Hamburg tracts that North Augusta acquired for $175,700 have remained dormant for more than a decade. The

In stark contrast to the Meriwether Monument, the ruins of Hamburg lay neglected and hidden in the woods on property owned by the City of North Augusta. *Courtesy the author.*

Located across the Savannah River from Hamburg, the Augusta Riverwalk includes several historical markers along the walking trail. *Courtesy the author.*

vision to construct a history trail dedicated to Hamburg's memory remains just that—a vision. It's tragic considering that directly across the Savannah River, the Augusta Riverwalk features a series of historical markers strategically placed along a nicely landscaped walking trail.

For most, Hamburg's ruins lie hidden in plain sight, waiting to be discovered. Perhaps one day they will be.

EPILOGUE

What makes the history of Hamburg so compelling is that, in many ways, this riverside hamlet embodied all that America represents, especially in relation to the Hamburg Massacre of 1876. Parallels between Hamburg and current events are painfully obvious.

This book has already delved into the Confederate-era monument debate that has unfolded in South Carolina and nationwide. Heritage versus hate arguments abound. This debate even became a campaign issue in the 2020 presidential election, with former president Donald J. Trump vetoing the Defense Authorization Bill because, among other things, the legislation called for renaming bases honoring Confederates.

And just when the Hamburg Massacre itself seemed like just another barbaric nineteenth-century event that couldn't possibly happen today, it did. On January 6, 2021, thousands of insurrectionists stormed the U.S. Capitol building, leading to the deaths of at least six people, including a police officer. Just as crusty ex-Confederates rebelled against Reconstruction, a cadre of QAnon adherents, white supremacists and other extremists rebelled against the certification of a presidential election they believed had been "stolen" from a modern-day Ben Tillman.

The chief difference today is that democracy prevailed. Democracy defeated crooked and corrupt attempts to undermine it. Yet the 2021 insurrection should remind Americans of one inescapable reality: democracy today is as fragile as it was in 1876.

Notes

Prologue

1. Shultz, "Memorial of Henry Shultz," 1.

Chapter 1

2. Crass, *Excavations at New Windsor Township*, 19–23.
3. Cashin, *Story of Augusta*, 5, 51, 71, 101–4.
4. Trinkley et al., *Cultural Resources Survey*, 8.
5. Cashin, *Story of Augusta*, 5; Crass, *Excavations at New Windsor Township*, 19.
6. Chapman, *History of Edgefield County*, 239.
7. Crass, *Excavations at New Windsor Township*, 19.
8. Prentice, "Southeast Chronicles."
9. Crass, *Excavations at New Windsor Township*, 22–23.
10. National Park Service, "Harris-Pearson-Walker House."
11. Cashin, *Story of Augusta*, 51.
12. Hammond and Hammond, "One Thousand Dollar Reward."
13. Chapman, *History of Edgefield County*, 239; Shaffer, "German Who Hated Augusta," 8.
14. Shaffer, "German Who Hated Augusta," 8.
15. Helsley, *Lost Aiken County*, 90; Moller, "Die Wundersame Geschichte."
16. Scott, *Random Recollections of a Long Life*, 26.
17. Bonner and Roberts, *Studies in Georgia History*, 79.

18. *Handbook of South Carolina*, "Commerce, Transportation and Immigration and Emigration," 478.
19. Rothbard, *Panic of 1819*, 7.
20. *Handbook of South Carolina*, "Commerce, Transportation and Immigration and Emigration," 478.
21. Scott, *Random Recollections of a Long Life*, 26.
22. "New Bridge."
23. *Handbook of South Carolina*, "Commerce, Transportation and Immigration and Emigration," 480.
24. *Hamburg Gazette*, July 21, 1824, 3.
25. *Handbook of South Carolina*, "Commerce, Transportation and Immigration and Emigration," 480.
26. Cashin, *Story of Augusta*, 72.
27. Bonner and Roberts, *Studies in Georgia History*, 79–81.
28. Cashin, *Story of Augusta*, 72; Bonner and Roberts, *Studies in Georgia History*, 79–80.
29. Cashin, *Story of Augusta*, 72.
30. Chapman, *History of Edgefield County*, 239.

Chapter 2

31. Bonner and Roberts, *Studies in Georgia History*, 80–81.
32. Chapman, *History of Edgefield County*, 237.
33. Scott, *Random Recollections of a Long Life*, 26–27.
34. Chapman, *History of Edgefield County*, 103.
35. Bonner and Roberts, *Studies in Georgia History*, 86.
36. Shultz, "Acts Speak Stronger than Words," 1.
37. Ibid.
38. Boles, *Origin of the Town of Hamburg*, 137.
39. Ibid., 138.
40. Burton, *In My Father's House*, 30.
41. *Handbook of South Carolina*, "Commerce, Transportation and Immigration and Emigration," 479.
42. Chapman, *History of Edgefield County*, 237.
43. "Story About Hamburg."
44. Chapman, *History of Edgefield County*, 237.
45. Ibid., 240.
46. Ibid.; Scott, *Random Recollections of a Long Life*, 27.
47. "Prices, Current Exchange."
48. "Arrived."
49. "Notice."

50. Ibid.
51. Bonner and Roberts, *Studies in Georgia History*, 80.
52. *Handbook of South Carolina*, "Commerce, Transportation and Immigration and Emigration," 479; Bonner and Roberts, *Studies in Georgia History*, 80. The *Handbook* notes that the wharf opened in 1816, while Bonner and Roberts peg the year at 1817.
53. *Handbook of South Carolina*, "Commerce, Transportation and Immigration and Emigration," 479.
54. Bonner and Roberts, *Studies in Georgia History*, 80.
55. Ibid., 82.
56. Ibid., 89.
57. *Handbook of South Carolina*, "Commerce, Transportation and Immigration and Emigration," 479.

Chapter 3

58. Taylor, "Hamburg," 21.
59. Bonner and Roberts, *Studies in Georgia History*, 92.
60. Blanding, *Report on the Practicality of Constructing*, 1–2.
61. Ibid., 3.
62. Robertson, *Journal of the Brotherhood of Locomotive Engineers*, 524.
63. Blanding, *Report on the Practicality of Constructing*, 3.
64. Wayt, "Railroad Tracks Belonging," 20.
65. Ibid.
66. Fetters, *Charleston & Hamburg*, 46.
67. Wayt, "Railroad Tracks Belonging," 20–21.
68. Ibid., 19.
69. Ibid., 21.
70. Ibid., 34.
71. Grier, "South Carolina Rail Road," 36.
72. Robertson, *Journal of the Brotherhood of Locomotive Engineers*, 524.
73. Wayt, "Railroad Tracks Belonging," 22.
74. "Railroad to Retain Aiken 'Cut.'"
75. "American Independence."
76. Town Council of Aiken, "Petition for Increased Power."
77. Downey, *Planting a Capitalist South*, 111.
78. Lossing, *Pictorial Fieldbook of the Revolution*, vol. 2, 503.
79. "Story About Hamburg"; Chapman, *History of Edgefield County*, 238.
80. *Handbook of South Carolina*, "Commerce, Transportation and Immigration and Emigration," 479.

81. "From the Chronicle & Sentinel."
82. Fetters, *Charleston & Hamburg*, 88.
83. Wayt, "Railroad Tracks Belonging," 20.
84. "Curious Animal."
85. "Ladies Fair, and Fair Ladies."
86. Chapman, *History of Edgefield County*, 242–43.
87. Taylor, "Hamburg," 30.
88. Burton, *In My Father's House*, 39.

Chapter 4

89. Scott, *Random Recollections of a Long Life*, 27.
90. Chapman, *History of Edgefield County*, 239.
91. "Augusta."
92. Bonner and Roberts, *Studies in Georgia History*, 91.
93. "Augusta."
94. "Forensic Display."
95. National Archives and History, "Kansas-Nebraska Act (1854)."
96. U.S. Congress, "Butler, Andrew Pickens."
97. Chapman, *History of Edgefield County*, 110.
98. Scott, *Random Recollections of a Long Life*, 28.
99. Bonner and Roberts, *Studies in Georgia History*, 88.
100. *Edgefield Advertiser*, March 26, 1845.
101. Chapman, *History of Edgefield County*, 104.
102. "Manufactures in Augusta."
103. "Savannah River."
104. "Hamburg—Her Prospects," also with excerpts from the *Charleston Daily News*.
105. "Bridge Case."
106. "Our Town—Its Prospects."
107. *Journal of the House of Representatives*, 1865; South Carolina General Assembly, "General Orders of the Day," 177
108. City of North Augusta, "History of North Augusta."
109. South Carolina General Assembly, *Acts and Joint Resolutions*, 600; "Negroes Wanted."
110. Downey, *Planting a Capitalist South*, 188.
111. "Penny Wise and Pound Foolish."
112. "Our Plank Roads."
113. "Hamburg & Edgefield Plank Road!," October 30, 1851.
114. "Trip to Augusta."
115. "Edgefield & Hamburg Plank Road," August 13, 1856.

116. "Hamburg & Edgefield Plank Road," April 7, 1858.
117. Downey, *Planting a Capitalist South*, 188–89.

Chapter 5

118. Chapman, *History of Edgefield County*, 20.
119. *Edgefield Advertiser*, August 14, 1861, 5; November 20, 1861, 4; March 25, 1863.
120. "Tax Assessor's Notice."
121. "Edgefield Rangers"; "To Horse! To Horse!"; Family Tree and Family History—Geni, "Maj. Andrew J. Hammond."
122. "Edgefield Rangers," 3.
123. Benson, *Berry Benson's Civil War Book*, 1.
124. Ibid., 175.
125. "Very Warlike."
126. "Camp Near Mathew's Bluff."
127. "Gov. Bonham's Message."
128. American Battlefield Trust, "Scorched Earth."
129. "From Savannah."
130. Murray, "General Sherman, The Negro, and Slavery," 125–30.
131. "Columbia and Hamburg R.R."
132. "Negroes Wanted."
133. "Destructive Fire in Hamburg."
134. "Fire in Hamburg"; "Destructive Fire in Hamburg."
135. "Another Incendiary Fire."
136. "Flood at Augusta."
137. "Great Flood."
138. "Who Blames Them?"
139. Hill, "New Spring Stock."
140. "Pulled Up Stakes."
141. *Southern Enterprise*, March 18, 1868.
142. "Fire in Hamburg."
143. Chapman, *History of Edgefield County*, 104.

Chapter 6

144. U.S. Senate, *South Carolina in 1876*, 38, testimony of Dock Adams.
145. Higginson, *Army Life in a Black Regiment*, 57.
146. "Struggle of '76."
147. U.S. Senate, *South Carolina in 1876*, 38, testimony of Dock Adams.
148. Higginson, *Army Life in a Black Regiment*, 57.

149. S.A.T., untitled article, *Southern Enterprise*, March 18, 1868, 1.
150. "Poor Old Hamburg!"
151. Ibid.
152. "Hamburg and Augusta War."
153. "Another War Brewing."
154. "Specimen Carolina."
155. "Hamburg and Augusta War."
156. Williams, untitled article, *Daily Phoenix*, March 17, 1871, 2.
157. U.S. Senate, *South Carolina in 1876*, 37–38, testimony of Dock Adams.

Chapter 7

158. U.S. Senate, *South Carolina in 1876*, 309, testimony of Thomas Butler.
159. Ibid., 308–9.
160. Budiansky, *Bloody Shirt*, 226.
161. "Not Guilty."
162. "Edgefield Disturbance." Reverend J.P. Mealing was among those signing a letter along with M.C. Butler and Ben Tillman condemning Ned Tenant and his black militia.
163. U.S. Senate, *South Carolina in 1876*, 75, testimony of Dock Adams.
164. "Owre True Tale."
165. U.S. Senate, *South Carolina in 1876*, 218, testimony of John Lee.
166. National Register of Historic Places, "Georgia Avenue—Butler Avenue Historic District," Nomination Form, 2.
167. "Trouble at Ridge Springs."
168. "Gossip with Our Exchanges."
169. "Edgefield Troubles"; "Serious Trouble in Edgefield County"; "Disturbance in Edgefield."
170. "Troubles in Edgefield."
171. "Serious Trouble in Edgefield County."
172. "Edgefield Quiet."
173. "Troubles in Edgefield."
174. "Edgefield—Judge Mackey."
175. "Edgefield Trouble—The Report of Judge Mackey to the Governor."
176. "Gossip with Our Exchanges."
177. "Two Generals."
178. "Interview with Prince Rivers."

Chapter 8

179. "Heads Broken, Throats Cut."
180. "Atonement."
181. "Preparing for War in Edgefield."
182. "Death and Sketch of W.H.H. Butler."
183. Ibid.
184. U.S. Senate, *South Carolina in 1876*, 308, testimony of Thomas Butler.
185. Ibid., 319–20.
186. "What Bloodhounds Can Do."
187. "New Feature."
188. U.S. Senate, *South Carolina in 1876*, 324–39, testimony of Henry Getzen.
189. Ibid., 1,052, testimony of R.J. Butler.

Chapter 9

190. U.S. Senate, *South Carolina in 1876*, 146, testimony of Louis Schiller.
191. Ibid., 35–36, testimony of Dock Adams.
192. Ibid., 497–98, testimony of Henry Sparnick.
193. "Result in Edgefield."
194. U.S. Senate, *South Carolina in 1876*, 220, testimony of John Lee,
195. Ibid., 3, testimony of Jerry Thornton Moore.
196. Ibid., 376–77, testimony of James Kennedy.
197. Ibid., 374–75.
198. Ibid., 606–7, testimony of William Nelson.
199. Ibid., 714, testimony of Samuel Spencer.
200. Ibid., 704, testimony of John Williams.
201. Ibid., 310, testimony of Thomas Butler.
202. Ibid., 308–23, testimony of Thomas Butler; 324–39, testimony of Henry Getzen.
203. U.S. Senate, *South Carolina in 1876*, 146, testimony of Louis Schiller.
204. Ibid., 1,063, testimony of J.P. Mealing.

Chapter 10

205. Ibid., 490, testimony of Henry Sparnick.
206. *Journal of the House of Representatives*, 1865, 7.
207. *Daily Phoenix*, October 8, 1870, 2; *Daily Phoenix*, October 9, 1870, 2; "Asylum Job Again."
208. "Local Affairs," September 5, 1874; "Railroad Meeting"; "Aiken's Journalism."

209. "Aiken's Journalism."
210. "Henry Sparnick Endorsement."
211. "Sparnick Trial."
212. "Put Up or Shut Up."
213. U.S. Senate, *South Carolina in 1876*, 490–91, testimony of Henry Sparnick.
214. Ibid., 1,054, testimony of Robert J. Butler.
215. Ibid., 1,053, testimony of Robert J. Butler; 1,063–64, testimony of J.P. Mealing; 1,058, testimony of H.A. Shaw.
216. U.S. Senate, *South Carolina in 1876*, 327, testimony of Henry Getzen; "Truth About Hamburg."
217. U.S. Senate, *South Carolina in 1876*, 37, testimony of Dock Adams.
218. Ibid., 1,064–65, testimony of J.P. Mealing.
219. "Truth About Hamburg."
220. "Struggle of '76."

Chapter 11

221. U.S. Senate, *South Carolina in 1876*, 710, testimony of Samuel Spencer.
222. Ginsberg, *Moses of South Carolina*, 73.
223. Brooks, *Butler and His Cavalry*, 52–53.
224. Brooks, *Initial Historic Overview*, 65.
225. Morgan, *Recollections of a Rebel Reefer*, 370–74.
226. U.S. Senate, *South Carolina in 1876*, 603, testimony of William Nelson.

Chapter 12

227. Ibid., 38, testimony of Dock Adams.
228. Ibid., 491, 493–94, testimony of Henry Sparnick. Butler's reference to his "cousin" may not have indicated a literal familial connection, as historical sources vary on this.
229. Ibid., 492–93.
230. Ibid., 710, testimony of Samuel Spencer.
231. Ibid., 40, testimony of Dock Adams.
232. Ibid., 161, testimony of Needham O'Bryant; 713, testimony of Samuel Spencer.
233. U.S. Senate, *South Carolina in 1876*, 239, testimony of General M.C. Butler.
234. Ibid., 241–42.
235. Ibid., 39, testimony of Dock Adams.
236. Ibid., 31, testimony of Harry Mays; 149, testimony of Louis Schiller.
237. U.S. Senate, *South Carolina in 1876*, 86, testimony of Samuel Picksley.

238. Ibid., 39, testimony of Dock Adams.
239. Ibid., 40, testimony of Dock Adams; 80, testimony of Samuel Picklsey.

Chapter 13

240. U.S. Senate, *South Carolina in 1876*, 604, testimony of William Nelson.
241. Ibid., 611–12, testimony of Franklin Robinson.
242. Ibid., 614, testimony of Spencer Harris.
243. Ibid., 40, testimony of Dock Adams.
244. Ibid., 42.
245. "Struggle of '76."
246. Butler, "M'Kie Meriwether"; "Hamburg Tragedy."
247. U.S. Senate, *South Carolina in 1876*, 331, testimony of Henry Getzen.
248. Ibid., 243, testimony of General M.C. Butler.
249. "Struggle of '76."
250. U.S. Senate, *South Carolina in 1876*, 41, testimony of Dock Adams.
251. Ibid., 32, testimony of Henry Mays; "After the Battle."
252. "After the Battle"; "Hamburg Tragedy."
253. U.S. Senate, *South Carolina in 1876*, 42, testimony of Dock Adams; "Struggle of '76."
254. U.S. Senate, *South Carolina in 1876*, 33, testimony of Harry Mays; 697, testimony of Archie Griffin; 711, testimony of Samuel Spencer; "Truth About Hamburg."
255. U.S. Senate, *South Carolina in 1876*, 42, testimony of Dock Adams; "Struggle of '76."
256. U.S. Senate, *South Carolina in 1876*, 43, testimony of Dock Adams.
257. Ibid., 604, testimony of William Nelson.
258. Ibid., 43, testimony of Dock Adams; "Truth About Hamburg."

Chapter 14

259. U.S. House of Representatives, "Massacre of Six Colored Citizens," 2.
260. Stone, *Attorney General Stone's Report*.
261. "Great Riot in Hamburg"; "Hamburg Row"; Pettit, "Recommendations Regarding the Meriwether Monument," 8.
262. "Local Affairs," July 29, 1876.
263. "Truth About Hamburg."
264. U.S. Senate, *South Carolina in 1876*, 33–34, testimony of Harry Mays.
265. Ibid., 526–27, testimony of John Freyer.
266. Ibid., 526, testimony of John Freyer; 34, testimony of Harry Mays; 44–45, testimony of Dock Adams. Only Dock Adams testified that it was General M.C. Butler who personally called Attaway's name in the dead ring.
267. U.S. Senate, *South Carolina in 1876*, 34, testimony of Harry Mays.

268. U.S. House of Representatives, "Massacre of Six Colored Citizens," 2.
269. Chapman, *History of Edgefield County*, 261.
270. U.S. Senate, *South Carolina in 1876*, 527, testimony of John Freyer.
271. Stone, *Attorney General Stone's Report.*
272. "Struggle of '76."
273. U.S. Senate, *South Carolina in 1876*, 34, testimony of Harry Mays.
274. Ibid., 527, testimony of John Freyer.
275. Ibid., 34, testimony of Harry Mays.
276. Ibid., 45, testimony of Dock Adams.
277. Ibid., 527, testimony of John Freyer.
278. Ibid., 45, testimony of Dock Adams.
279. Ibid., 605, testimony of William Nelson.
280. "Struggle of '76."
281. U.S. Senate, *South Carolina in 1876*, 151–52, testimony of Louis Schiller.

Chapter 15

282. "After the Battle"; "Hamburg Tragedy."
283. U.S. Senate, *South Carolina in 1876*, 605, testimony of William Nelson.
284. U.S. House of Representatives, "Massacre of Six Colored Citizens," 2.
285. Ibid., 7.
286. South Carolina General Assembly, "White Man's Revolution," 747.
287. "Aiken's Town Halls." Lyceum Hall was later torn down and replaced by the May Building, which according to Aiken County property records was built in 1932. Today, the building serves as the location of What's Cookin' Downtown, a popular eatery on Laurens Street.
288. "Hamburg Riot Cases."
289. South Carolina General Assembly, "White Man's Revolution," 747; "Truth About Hamburg."
290. Creelman, "Defender of the Senate," 628.
291. Hemphill, *Men of Mark in South Carolina*, 164.
292. Butler, "Hamburg Collision."
293. Thomson, "Election of Angus Cameron," 195–200.
294. Moore, "Isaac Peckham Christiancy," 231–34.
295. "Southern Campaign."
296. U.S. Senate, *South Carolina in 1876*, 922–23, statement by Senator Augustus Merrimon.
297. "Dual Governments."
298. "Carolina's Choice."
299. U.S. House of Representatives, "Massacre of Six Colored Citizens," 18.

300. "Hamburg Coroner."
301. "Local Affairs," March 15, 1877.

Chapter 16

302. "Hamburg Militiaman Gets Five Hundred Dollars."
303. "South Carolina News," February 20, 1879.
304. Budiansky, *Bloody Shirt*, 253; Holt, *Black Over White*, 80.
305. "General Prince Rivers."
306. Moore, *South Carolina Newspapers*, 7.
307. "State News," September 12, 1877.
308. "Aiken Journal."
309. "State News," December 2, 1886.
310. *Journal and Review*, October 26, 1892.
311. U.S. Senate, *South Carolina in 1876*, 47–48, 76, testimony of Dock Adams.
312. "Dock Adams Dead."
313. Citizens of Hamburg, *Petition Against the Repeal of the Hamburg Town Charter.*
314. "Some of the Work of the Legislature."

Chapter 17

315. Headley, *Public Men of To-day*, 108.
316. Creelman, "Defender of the Senate," 625.
317. Ibid., 629.
318. Simkins, *Pitchfork Ben Tillman*, 173.
319. "Hamburg Redeemed."
320. Simkins, *Pitchfork Ben Tillman*, 234.
321. "Humbug in Hamburg."
322. "Departed Glories."
323. "Georgia and Florida."
324. Uptown, Municipal Association of South Carolina, "Home Rule."
325. "Barely Missed It."
326. "Local Items."
327. "List of the Acts and Joint Resolutions Passed," 1; "Historic Hamburg to Be Rejuvenated."
328. "Edgefield Man Heads the Ticket in Aiken"; "Judge Getzen Shot."
329. "Judge Getzen Shot," 3; Kirby, "Getzen's Pond Was Place for Swimming."
330. "Judge Getzen Dead!"
331. "What Bloodhounds Can Do."

332. "New Feature."
333. "Battle at Hamburg."
334. "Not Guilty."
335. "Shotgun Duel at Hamburg."
336. "Bloody Battle Waged."
337. Ibid.
338. "Battle at Hamburg."
339. Ibid.
340. Ibid.
341. "Local Brevities," June 22 and July 6, 1893.
342. "Not Guilty."
343. "Death and Sketch of W.H.H. Butler."

Chapter 18

344. Helsley, *Lost Aiken County*, 86, 111.
345. "North Augusta Incorporated."
346. National Oceanic & Atmospheric Administration, "Record of Climatological Observations."
347. "Cotton Crop."
348. "Richmond and Danville R.R. Co. South Carolina Division."
349. "South Carolina News," May 13, 1892.
350. "Hamburg in Ashes."
351. "Story About Hamburg."
352. "Departed Glories."
353. "Terrible Havoc Feared from Floods."
354. "Terrible Loss."
355. U.S. Geological Survey, *South Carolina Floods and Droughts*.
356. "Dam Above Augusta Breaks."
357. "Floods Raging in Piedmont."
358. Ibid.
359. "Damage at Augusta."
360. "Terrible Loss."
361. "Great Damage of Flood."
362. National Oceanic & Atmospheric Administration, "Calcium Oxide."
363. "Horror of the Augusta Flood."
364. "Terrible Loss."
365. Rowland and Callahan, *Yesterday's Augusta*, 39.
366. "Flood of 1796."
367. Rowland and Callahan, *Yesterday's Augusta*, 39; Trinkley, *Cultural Resources Survey*, 36.

368. Trinkley, *Cultural Resources Survey*, 36.
369. Ibid., 8.
370. Ibid., 9.
371. "Augusta's Greatest Fire."
372. "History of Hamburg."
373. Rowland and Callahan, *Yesterday's Augusta*, 39.
374. South Carolina Department of Natural Resources, "South Carolina Hurricanes."
375. "Floods Do Great Damage."
376. National Oceanic & Atmospheric Administration, "Record of Climatological Observations."
377. Tilson, *Augusta*, 31–32.
378. Landsea, *Reanalysis of the 1921–30 Atlantic Hurricane Database*, 880.
379. Barnes, *Florida's Hurricane History*, 73.
380. South Carolina Department of Natural Resources, "South Carolina Hurricanes."
381. National Oceanic & Atmospheric Administration, "Record of Climatological Observations."
382. "Nothing but Name Left at Hamburg."
383. "Epidemic May Follow When Flood Subsides."
384. "Red Cross Work in Hamburg Ends."
385. "Hamburg Must Go, States Red Cross."
386. "Red Cross Work in Hamburg Ends."
387. "Hamburg Problem Solution Planned."
388. Aiken County Government, Office of the Register of Mesne Conveyance, Deeds to 135 Sand Pit Road.
389. "Nothing but Name Left at Hamburg."

Chapter 19

390. "Unveil Monument to McKie Meriwether."
391. "McKie Meriwether Monument Completed."
392. Butler, "M'Kie Meriwether."
393. "Monument Erected in North Augusta."
394. South Carolina General Assembly, "White Man's Revolution," 741–42, 744, 748.
395. Ibid., 749, 751.
396. "Monument Erected."
397. "His First Speech Yielded Results."
398. Butler, "Col. A.P. Butler's Place in History"; Toole, "90 Years in Aiken County"; "Aiken's Panorama of 100 Years."

399. Kimball, "One Man's Fight"; South Carolina Picture Project, "Hamburg Massacre."
400. Britt, "Monumental Injustice?"; Britt, "Sad Reminder of a Dark Day."
401. "Editorial: Investing in the Future of NA"; Aiken County Government, Office of the Register of Mesne Conveyance, Deeds to 135 Sand Pit Road.
402. Pettit, interview by Michael Smith, February 9, 2020.
403. Pettit presentation, Calhoun Park Committee meeting.
404. Bengtson, "N. Augusta Council Approves Rezoning," 14.
405. Folker, "Black Victims of 1876 Hamburg Massacre."
406. Calhoun Park Committee meeting, Q&A Discussion.
407. South Carolina General Assembly, House, "SC Infantry Battle Flag."

Chapter 20

408. Mitchell, Unify North Augusta protest, North Augusta, South Carolina, June 20, 2020.
409. Cook and Jones, "Meriwether Monument Opinion."
410. Taylor, interview by Michael Smith.
411. Schechter, "After Weeks of Protests."
412. Young, interview by Michael Smith.
413. Hutt, North Augusta City Council meeting, public input.
414. Thomas, North Augusta City Council meeting, public input.
415. Charleston City Council, Resolution on the Relocation of John C. Calhoun Statue.
416. North Augusta City Council, "Resolution Providing Findings."
417. Mackie, "Meriwether Monument Committee Report to Council."
418. WRDW, "Timeline of Project Jackson."
419. Hodges, "North Augusta City Council."

Bibliography

Ackerman, Robert Kilgo. *Wade Hampton III*. Columbia: University of South Carolina Press, 2007.

"After the Battle." *Weekly Chronicle and Sentinel*, Augusta, Georgia, July 19, 1876, 1.

Aiken County Government, Office of the Register of Mesne Conveyance. Deeds to 135 Sand Pit Road. www.acwebegs.aikencountysc.gov.

"Aiken Journal." *Anderson (SC) Intelligencer*, March 31, 1881.

"Aiken's Journalism." *Journal and Review*. Aiken, South Carolina, May 27, 1892.

"Aiken's Panorama of 100 Years." *Aiken (SC) Standard and Review*, August 28, 1967, 2C.

"Aiken's Town Halls." *Aiken (SC) Standard*, August 22, 1973.

"All Quiet in Edgefield." *Edgefield (SC) Advertiser*, September 26, 1874.

American Battlefield Trust. "Scorched Earth: Sherman's March to the Sea." www.battlefields.org.

"American Independence." *Aiken (SC) Telegraph and Commercial Advertiser*, July 8, 1835.

American Newspaper Directory. New York: Geo. P. Rowell & Company, Publishers, 1879.

"Another Incendiary Fire." *Edgefield (SC) Advertiser*, December 14, 1864.

"Another War Brewing." *Fairfield Herald*, Winnsboro, South Carolina, March 22, 1871.

"Arrived." *Hamburg Gazette*, July 23, 1823.

Ash, John, et al. "Citizens of Hamburg, Petition Protesting the Repeal of the Towns Charter." South Carolina Department of Archives & History, undated but circa 1877.

"The Asylum Job Again." *Daily Phoenix*, Columbia, SC, November 3, 1870.

"The Atonement." *Abbeville (SC) Press & Banner*, May 24, 1876.

"Augusta." *Augusta (GA) Chronicle and Commercial Advertiser*, August 8, 1827.

"Augusta Advertisements: Appointments." *Edgefield (SC) Advertiser*, October 31, 1872.

"Augusta's Greatest Fire." *Edgefield (SC) Advertiser*, June 8, 1899.

"Bahamas Severely Hit by Hurricane: South Menaced by Flood Rains." *Cornell Daily Sun*, Ithaca, NY, September 28, 1929.

"Barely Missed It." *Anderson (SC) Intelligencer*, July 25, 1894.

Barnes, Jay. *Florida's Hurricane History*. Chapel Hill: University of North Carolina Press, 1998.

"Battle at Hamburg: Three Out of Four Shot in a Hot Street Encounter." *Journal and Review*, Aiken, SC, May 31, 1893.

"The Bayonet in Politics." *Anderson (SC) Intelligencer*, August 27, 1876.

Bengtson, Bill. "N. Augusta Council Approves Rezoning." *North Augusta (SC) Star*, June 5, 2007.

Benson, Susan Williams, ed. *Berry Benson's Civil War Book: Memoirs of a Confederate Scout and Sharpshooter*. Athens: University of Georgia Press, 1991.

Berry, Stephen. "The Hamburg Massacre." CSI: Dixie. https://csidixie.org.

"Better Late than Never." *Courier-Journal*, Aiken, SC, July 29, 1876.

Blanding, Abram. *Report on the Practicality of Constructing a Canal or Railroad Between Charleston and Hamburgh*. South Carolina Department of Archives and History, March 15, 1828. www.archivesindex.sc.gov.

"Bloody Battle Waged." *Edgefield (SC) Advertiser*, June 1, 1893.

Boles, J. Durelle, collector. *Origin of the Town of Hamburg, South Carolina*. GEU: Benjamin Brantly printer. EMU10001453472. J. Durelle Boles Collection of Southern Imprints.

Bonner, James C., and Lucien E. Roberts. *Studies in Georgia History and Government*. Athens: University of Georgia Press, 1940.

"Bridge Case." *Edgefield (SC) Advertiser*, January 14, 1846.

Britt, Phyllis. "Monumental Injustice?" *Aiken (SC) Standard*, April 16, 2008, 1A, 14A.

———. "A Sad Reminder of a Dark Day." *Aiken (SC) Standard*, April 16, 2008, 15A.

Brooks, Richard D. *Initial Historic Overview of the Savannah River Plant, Aiken and Barnwell Counties, South Carolina*. Columbia: University of South Carolina Press, 1981.

Brooks, U.R. *Butler and His Cavalry in the War of Secession: 1861–1865*. Columbia, SC: State Company, 1909.

Budiansky, Stephen. *The Bloody Shirt: Terror After Appomattox*. New York: Viking, 2008.

Burton, Orville Vernon. *In My Father's House Are Many Mansions: Family and Community in Edgefield, South Carolina*. 3rd printing. Chapel Hill: University of North Carolina Press, 1988.

Butler, F.W.P. "Col. A.P. Butler's Place in History." *Edgefield (SC) Advertiser*, January 25, 1922.

Butler, M.C. "Gen. Butler Strikes Back." *Abbeville (SC) Press & Banner*, July 26, 1872.

———. "General Butler's History of the Affair." *News & Times*, Orangeburg, SC, July 15, 1876.
———. "The Hamburg Collision." *Anderson (SC) Intelligencer*, July 20, 1876.
Butler, W.W.P. "M'Kie Meriwether." *The State*, Columbia, SC, January 23, 1914.
Calhoun Park Committee. Meeting, Q&A Discussion. Providence Baptist Church, North Augusta, SC, February 9, 2020.
"A Call for Federal Troops." *Lexington (SC) Dispatch*, October 7, 1874.
"Camp Near Mathew's Bluff." *Edgefield (SC) Advertiser*, January 25, 1865.
"Carolina's Choice: Her New Senator, General M.C. Butler." *News and Herald*, Winnsboro, SC, January 4, 1877.
Cashin, Edward J. *The Story of Augusta*. Augusta, GA: Richmond County Board of Education, 1980.
Chapman, John. *History of Edgefield County from the Earliest Settlements to 1897*. Newberry, SC: Elbert H. Aull, Publisher and Printer, 1897.
Charleston City Council. Resolution on the Relocation of John C. Calhoun Statue. Resolution adopted June 23, 2020.
"The Charleston Negroes on the 'Hamburg Massacre.'" *Anderson (SC) Intelligencer*, August 27, 1876.
Citizens of Hamburg. *Petition Against the Repeal of the Hamburg Town Charter.* South Carolina Department of Archives and History, June 1877.
City of North Augusta. "History of North Augusta." https://www.northaugusta.net.
"Columbia and Hamburg R.R." *Edgefield (SC) Advertiser*, June 6, 1865.
Cook, Robert D., and David S. Jones. "Meriwether Monument Opinion." South Carolina Attorney General's Office, Columbia, SC, July 21, 2020.
"The Cotton Crop." *Yorkville (SC) Enquirer*, May 13, 1891.
Crass, David Colin. *Excavations at New Windsor Township, South Carolina*. Columbia: University of South Carolina Press, 1997.
Creelman, James. "A Defender of the Senate." *Pearson's Magazine* (December 31, 1906).
"A Curious Animal." *Kershaw (SC) Gazette*, May 3, 1883.
Daily Phoenix. Columbia, South Carolina, October 8–9, 1870, 2.
"Dam Above Augusta Breaks." *Fort Mill (SC) Times*, September 11, 1908.
"The Damage at Augusta." *Watchman and Southron*, Sumter, South Carolina, September 2, 1908.
"Death and Sketch of W.H.H. Butler." *Greenwood (SC) Daily Journal*, August 14, 1901.
"Departed Glories." *Edgefield (SC) Advertiser*, December 1, 1892.
"Destructive Fire in Hamburg." *Edgefield (SC) Advertiser*, January 18, 1865.
"Destructive Fire in Hamburg." *Edgefield (SC) Advertiser*, November 23, 1865.
"The Disturbance in Edgefield." *Camden (SC) Journal*, September 8, 1874.
"Dock Adams Dead." *Yorkville (SC) Enquirer*, September 10, 1898.

Downey, Tom. *Planting a Capitalist South: Masters, Merchants and Manufacturers in the Southern Interior, 1790 to 1860*. Baton Rouge: Louisiana State University Press, 2006.

"The Dual Governments." *Anderson (SC) Intelligencer*, January 18, 1877.

"Edgefield & Hamburg Plank Road." *Edgefield (SC) Advertiser*, August 13, 1856.

"The Edgefield Disturbance." *Anderson (SC) Intelligencer*, October 8, 1874.

"Edgefield—Judge Mackey." *Daily Phoenix*, Columbia, South Carolina, January 29, 1875.

"An Edgefield Man Heads the Ticket in Aiken." *Edgefield (SC) Advertiser*, August 24, 1882.

"Edgefield Quiet." *Newberry (SC) Herald*, September 30, 1874.

"The 'Edgefield Rangers.'" *Edgefield (SC) Advertiser*, August 7, 1861.

Edgefield (SC) Advertiser. March 26, 1845, 2. Originally published in the *Hamburg Republican*.

"The Edgefield Troubles." *Daily Phoenix*, Columbia, SC, September 26, 1874.

"The Edgefield Trouble—The Report of Judge Mackey to the Governor." *Daily Phoenix*, Columbia, South Carolina, January 30, 1875.

"Editorial: Investing in the Future of NA." *North Augusta (SC) Star*, October 10, 2009. www.northaugustastar.com.

"Editorial Notes." *Anderson (SC) Intelligencer*, July 27, 1876.

"Epidemic May Follow When Flood Subsides." *Aiken (SC) Standard*, October 4, 1929.

Family Tree and Family History—Geni. "Maj. Andrew J. Hammond." https://www.geni.com.

Fetters, Thomas. *The Charleston & Hamburg: A South Carolina Railroad and an American Legacy*. Charleston, SC: The History Press, 2008.

"Fire in Hamburg." *Edgefield (SC) Advertiser*, December 14, 1864.

"Fire in Hamburg." *Edgefield (SC) Advertiser*, December 30, 1868.

"The Flood at Augusta." *Tri-Weekly Journal*, Camden, South Carolina, January 20, 1865.

"Flood Damage Running High; Aiken County Big Sufferer." *Journal and Review*, Aiken, SC, October 4, 1929.

"Flood of 1796." *Augusta (GA) Chronicle*, January 23, 1796.

"Floods Do Great Damage in Two Carolinas and Georgia." *McCormick (SC) Messenger*, August 23, 1928, 8.

"The Floods of Last Week." *Yorkville (SC) Enquirer*, September 19, 1888.

"Floods Raging in Piedmont." *Watchman and Southron*, Sumter, South Carolina, August 26, 1908.

Folker, James. "Black Victims of 1876 Hamburg Massacre Get Historical Marker." *Augusta (GA) Chronicle*, March 6, 2016.

"Forensic Display." *Sumter (SC) Banner*, February 20, 1850.

"From Savannah." *Edgefield (SC) Advertiser*, January 18, 1865.

"From the Chronicle & Sentinel." *Edgefield (SC) Advertiser*, February 21, 1839. Originally published in the *Augusta Chronicle & Sentinel.*

"The Fury of the Floods." *Fairfield News and Herald*, Winnsboro, SC, September 19, 1888.

"Fury of the Floods." *Newberry (SC) Herald and News*, September 20, 1888.

"General Prince Rivers: His Death in Aiken; A Short Sketch of His Eventful Life." *Journal and Review*, Aiken, SC, April 20, 1887.

"Georgia and Florida." *Morning News*, Savannah, GA, October 12, 1892.

Ginsberg, Benjamin. *Moses of South Carolina: A Jewish Scalawag during Reconstruction.* Baltimore, MD: Johns Hopkins University Press, 2010.

"A Good Beginning." *Charleston (SC) Daily News*, May 30, 1871.

"Gossip with Our Exchanges." *Edgefield (SC) Advertiser*, December 1, 1875.

"Gov. Bonham's Message." *Edgefield (SC) Advertiser*, December 7, 1864.

"Great Damage of Flood." *Bamberg (SC) Herald*, September 3, 1908.

"The Great Flood: Augusta and Hamburg Submerged." *Edgefield (SC) Advertiser*, January 18, 1865.

"Great Freshet of the Savannah River!" *Edgefield (SC) Advertiser*, June 4, 1840.

"Great Riot in Hamburg." *Anderson (SC) Intelligencer*, July 13, 1876.

Grier, Robert. "South Carolina Rail Road." *The Georgia and Carolina Almanac for 1835*. N.p.

"Gross Misconduct on the Part of the County Commissioners." *Edgefield (SC) Advertiser*, June 5, 1871.

"The Hamburg and Augusta War." *Keowee Courier*, Walhalla, South Carolina, March 24, 1871.

"The Hamburg & Edgefield Plank Road." *Edgefield (SC) Advertiser*, April 7, 1858.

"Hamburg & Edgefield Plank Road!" *Edgefield (SC) Advertiser*, October 30, 1851.

"The Hamburg Coroner." *Anderson (SC) Intelligencer*, July 20, 1876.

"Hamburg—Her Prospects, etc." *Edgefield (SC) Advertiser*, August 22, 1849.

"Hamburg in Ashes: A Disastrous Fire in Augusta's Carolina Suburb." *Herald and News*, Newberry, SC, May 14, 1891.

"The Hamburg Militiaman Gets Five Hundred Dollars." *Anderson (SC) Intelligencer*, September 9, 1878.

"Hamburg Must Go, States Red Cross." *Aiken (SC) Standard*, November 22, 1929.

"Hamburg Problem Solution Planned." *Journal and Review*, December 11, 1929.

"Hamburg Redeemed." *Manning (SC) Times*, April 15, 1891.

"The Hamburg Riot Cases." *Courier-Journal*, Aiken, SC, August 12, 1876.

"Hamburg Row." *Orangeburg (SC) News & Times*, July 13, 1876.

Hamburg (SC) Gazette. July 21, 1824, 3.

"The Hamburg Tragedy." *Weekly Chronicle and Sentinel*, Augusta, Georgia, July 19, 1876, 1.

Hammond, S., and LeRoy Hammond. "One Thousand Dollar Reward." *Augusta (GA) Herald*, June 18, 1800, classified ad.

Handbook of South Carolina. "Commerce, Transportation, and Immigration and Emigration." 2nd ed. Columbia, SC: State Department of Agriculture, Commerce and Immigration, 1908.

Headley, Phineas Camp. *Public Men of To-day*. Hartford, CT: S.S. Scranton and Company, 1882.

"Heads Broken, Throats Cut." *Abbeville (SC) Press & Banner*, May 24, 1876.

Helsley, Alexia. *Lost Aiken County*. Charleston, SC: The History Press, 2019.

Hemphill, James Calvin. *Men of Mark in South Carolina: Ideals of American Life*. N.p.: Men of Mark Publishing Company, 1907.

"Henry Sparnick Endorsement." *Orangeburg (SC) News*, June 6, 1874.

Higginson, Thomas W. *Army Life in a Black Regiment*. Boston: Osgood & Company, 1870.

Hill, William. "New Spring Stock." *Edgefield (SC) Advertiser*, October 9, 1867.

"His First Speech Yielded Results." *Edgefield (SC) Advertiser*, March 11, 1914.

"Historic Hamburg to Be Rejuvenated." *Lancaster (SC) Enterprise*, September 2, 1903.

"History of Hamburg." *Bamberg (SC) Herald*, April 6, 1922.

Hodges, Lindsey. "North Augusta City Council to Vote on Amphitheater Fountain Funds." *North Augusta (SC) Star*, December 6, 2019. https://www.northaugustastar.com.

Holt, Thomas. *Black Over White: Negro Political Leadership in South Carolina during Reconstruction*. Urbana: University of Illinois Press, 1979.

"Horror of the Augusta Flood." *Times and Democrat*, Orangeburg, SC, September 1, 1908.

"Humbug in Hamburg." *Weekly Union (SC) Times*, June 17, 1892.

Hutt, Louis. North Augusta City Council meeting, public input. North Augusta, SC, June 15, 2020.

"Interview with Prince Rivers." *Weekly Constitutionalist*. Augusta, GA, September 1, 1875.

Journal of the House of Representatives of South Carolina. Extra Session of 1865, October 25, 1865.

"Judge Getzen Dead!" *Journal and Review*, Aiken, SC, November 10, 1920.

"Judge Getzen Shot." *Edgefield (SC) Advertiser*, January 6, 1897.

Kimball, Whitney. "One Man's Fight to Reclaim a Racist South Carolina Monument." Curbed, November 4, 2015. https://www.curbed.com.

Kirby, Bill. "Getzen's Pond Was Place for Swimming." *Augusta (GA) Chronicle*, June 26, 2014.

"The Ladies Fair, and Fair Ladies—The Various Wonders of Inventive Genius—Great Success—Burlesques—Gyascutus, etc." *Southern Enterprise*, Greenville, South Carolina, February 28, 1867.

Landsea, Christopher W., et al. *A Reanalysis of the 1921–30 Atlantic Hurricane Database.* National Oceanic and Atmospheric Administration, Silver Spring, Maryland, February 1, 2012.

Lee, W.A. "The Hamburg Affair in Congress." *Abbeville (SC) Press & Banner,* July 26, 1876.

"List of the Acts and Joint Resolutions Passed at the Regular Session and Approved by the Governor." *Keowee Courier,* Walhalla, SC, January 8, 1880.

"Local Affairs." *Aiken (SC) Courier-Journal,* July 29, 1876.

"Local Affairs." *Aiken (SC) Courier-Journal,* March 15, 1877.

"Local Affairs." *Aiken (SC) Courier-Journal,* September 5, 1874.

"Local Brevities." *Edgefield (SC) Advertiser,* June 22 and July 6, 1893.

"Local Items." *Edgefield (SC) Advertiser,* July 25, 1878.

Lossing, B.J. *Pictorial Fieldbook of the Revolution.* Vol. 2. New York: Harper Brothers, 1852.

MacDowell, Dorothy. "Aiken's Town Halls." *Aiken (SC) Standard,* August 22, 1973.

Mackie, Trina, Calhoun Park Committee member. Calhoun Park Committee meeting. Providence Baptist Church, North Augusta, SC, February 9, 2020.

———. "Meriwether Monument Committee Report to Council." North Augusta City Council meeting. North Augusta, SC, August 10, 2020.

"Manufactures in Augusta." *Edgefield (SC) Advertiser,* April 9, 1845.

"McKie Meriwether Monument Completed. Inscription Given in Full." *Edgefield (SC) Advertiser,* January 26, 1916.

"Meriwether Descendent Finds Black Cousin, Both Fight for Monument Removal." WJBF NewsChannel 6. Augusta, GA, June 22, 2020.

Mitchell, Brandy. Unify North Augusta protest, North Augusta, South Carolina, June 20, 2020.

Moller, Jurgen. "Die Wundersame Geschichte des Stadtebauers Henry Schultz alias Klaus Hinrich Klahn." https://www.wirliebendahme.de.

Monk, John. "SC Prosecutor Won't Bring Charges Against Sumter Officers After Man Shot 19 Times." *The State,* Columbia, SC, April 26, 2017.

"Monument Erected in North Augusta to Memory of Hero Who Lost Life in Hamburg Riot." *Edgefield (SC) Advertiser,* February 23, 1916.

Moore, John Hammond. *South Carolina Newspapers.* Columbia: University of South Carolina Press, 1988.

Moore, Joseph B. "Isaac Peckham Christiancy." *Michigan Law Review* 5, no. 4 (1907): 231–34. JSTOR, www.jstor.org/stable/1272955.

Morgan, James Morris. *Recollections of a Rebel Reefer: A Midshipman in Gray.* Boston: Houghton Mifflin Company, 1917.

Murray, Robert K. "General Sherman, The Negro, and Slavery: The Story of an Unrecognized Rebel." *Negro History Bulletin* 22, no. 6 (1959): 125–30. JSTOR.

National Archives and History. "Kansas-Nebraska Act (1854)." https://www.ourdocuments.gov.

National Oceanic & Atmospheric Administration. "Calcium Oxide," data sheet, March 20, 2019. https://cameochemicals.noaa.gov.

———. "Record of Climatological Observations." http://www.ncei.noaa.gov.

National Park Service. "Harris-Pearson-Walker House." https://www.nps.gov.

National Register of Historic Places, U.S. Department of the Interior. "Georgia Avenue—Butler Avenue Historic District." Inventory Nomination Form, March 9, 1984.

Neely, Wayne. *The Great Bahamas Hurricane of 1929: The Story of the Greatest Bahamian Hurricane of the Twentieth Century*. N.p.: iUniverse, 2013.

"Negroes Wanted." *Edgefield (SC) Advertiser*, February 1, 1865.

"Negro Troubles in Georgia." *Aiken (SC) Courier-Journal*, September 28, 1875.

"New Bridge." *Augusta (GA) Chronicle*, August 18, 1814.

"A New Feature—In Regard to the Hamburg Riot." *Edgefield (SC) Advertiser*, October 2, 1879.

North Augusta City Council. "Recommendations Regarding the Meriwether Monument in J.C. Calhoun Park." Presentation of Mayor Bob Pettit. North Augusta, SC, November 12, 2018.

———. "Resolution Providing Findings about the Hamburg Incident of 1876." North Augusta, SC, March 18, 2019.

"North Augusta Incorporated." *Journal and Review*, Aiken, SC, April 19, 1906.

"Not Guilty: This Is the Jury's Verdict About Tom Butler To-Day." *Edgefield (SC) Advertiser*, October 5, 1893.

"Nothing but Name Left at Hamburg." *Camden (SC) Chronicle*, November 1, 1929.

"Notice." *Carolina Galaxy and Commercial Advocate*, Hamburg, SC, October 4, 1834.

O'Bryant, Wayne, speaker. Calhoun Park Committee. Providence Baptist Church, North Augusta, SC, February 9, 2020.

"Our Plank Roads." *Edgefield (SC) Advertiser*, November 30, 1853.

"Our Town—Its Prospects." *Edgefield (SC) Advertiser*, October 10, 1849.

"An Owre True Tale: A Detective Who Worked for Reputation." *Orangeburg (SC) News & Times*, January 27, 1877.

"Penny Wise and Pound Foolish." *Edgefield (SC) Advertiser*, February 16, 1853. Originally published in the *Cheraw Chronicle*.

Pettit, Bob. "Recommendations Regarding the Meriwether Monument in J.C. Calhoun Park." City of North Augusta, November 2018.

"Poor Old Hamburg!" *Edgefield (SC) Advertiser*, March 9, 1871.

Prentice, Guy. "Southeast Chronicles: Ninety Six National Historic Site." National Park Service, 2003, Image 4. https://www.nps.gov.

"Preparing for War in Edgefield." *Union (SC) Daily Times*, June 23, 1876.

"Prices, Current Exchange." *Hamburg Gazette*, July 23, 1823.

Pritchard, William H. Column. *Carolina Galaxy and Commercial Advocate*, Hamburg, SC, October 4, 1834.

"Pulled Up Stakes and Moved Across the Savannah." *Edgefield (SC) Advertiser*, October 20, 1869.

"Put Up or Shut Up." *Orangeburg (SC) Times*, December 5, 1874.

"Railroad Meeting." *Anderson (SC) Intelligencer*, October 29, 1874.

"Railroad to Retain Aiken 'Cut.'" *Aiken (SC) Standard*, March 15, 1970.

"Rains and Floods Do Much Damage." *Barnwell (SC) People-Sentinel*, October 2, 1929.

"Red Cross Work in Hamburg Ends." *Aiken (SC) Journal and Review*, February 5, 1930.

"Remarks of G.W. Landrum, Esq." *Edgefield (SC) Advertiser*, January 30, 1856.

"The Result in Edgefield." *Charleston (SC) Daily News*, October 26, 1870.

Richardson, Charles H. "Opinion Referenced the Provisions of S.C. Code Ann. § 10-1-165. Specifically, Concerning the Propriety of the City of North Augusta's Attempted Actions." South Carolina Attorney General's Office, Columbia, SC, December 13, 2004. http://www.scag.gov.

"Richmond and Danville R.R. Co. South Carolina Division. Passenger Department." *Yorkville (SC) Enquirer*, May 6, 1891.

Robertson, J.W. *Journal of the Brotherhood of Locomotive Engineers* 28, no. 1 (January 1894).

Rothbard, Murray N. *The Panic of 1819: Reactions and Policies*. New York: Columbia University Press, 2002.

Rowland, Arthur Ray, and Helen Callahan. *Yesterday's Augusta*. Miami, FL: E.A. Seamann Publishing Inc., 1976.

S.A.T. Untitled article. *Southern Enterprise*, Greenville, South Carolina, March 18, 1868, 1.

Sanders, Curtis L., et al. *Flood Frequency of the Savannah River at Augusta, Georgia*. U.S. Geological Survey, Columbia, SC, 1990.

"Savannah River." *Edgefield (SC) Advertiser*, November 3, 1847.

Schechter, Maayan. "After Weeks of Protests, Columbia Lawmaker Says Ben Tillman Statue Should Be Removed." *The State*, Columbia, SC, June 9, 2020. https://www.thestate.com.

Scott, Edwin. *Random Recollections of a Long Life*. Columbia, SC: Charles A. Calvo Jr., Printer, 1884.

"Serious Trouble in Edgefield County." *Anderson (SC) Intelligencer*, October 1, 1874.

Shaffer, E.T.H. "German Who Hated Augusta Built Hamburg as Competition." *Journal and Review*, Aiken, SC, May 3, 1933.

"Shotgun Duel at Hamburg." *Anderson (SC) Intelligencer*, May 31, 1893.

Shultz, Henry. "Acts Speak Stronger than Words." *Columbia (SC) Telescope*, November 24, 1824.

———. "For the Advertiser." *Edgefield (SC) Advertiser*, February 6, 1840.

———. "Memorial of Henry Shultz." Letter to South Carolina legislature, January 29, 1821.

———. Op-ed. *Carolina Galaxy and Commercial Advocate*, Hamburg, SC, October 4, 1834.

Simkins, Francis Butler. *Pitchfork Ben Tillman.* Baton Rouge: Louisiana State University Press, 1944.

"Some of the Work of the Legislature." *Weekly Union (SC) Times*, June 15, 1877.

South Carolina Department of Natural Resources. "South Carolina Hurricanes." www.scwaterlaw.gov.

South Carolina General Assembly. *Acts and Joint Resolutions of the General Assembly of the State of South Carolina, Extra Session of 1877*. Vol. 16. N.p.: Calvo and Patton, State Printers, 1877.

———. *Acts and Joint Resolutions of the General Assembly of the State of South Carolina, Regular Session of 1893*. N.p.: Calvo and Patton, State Printers, 1893, 482.

———. *A Concurrent Resolution to Honor and Recognize the African-American Members of the South Carolina Executive, Legislative and Judicial Branches of Government*. 117th Session, March 13, 2007.

———. "General Orders of the Day." *Journal of the Senate* (December 19, 1849): 177.

———. South Carolina Code of Laws, Section 16-17-650. www.scstatehouse.gov.

———. "White Man's Revolution." *Journal of the Senate* (February 17, 1916): 741–42, 744, 748.

South Carolina General Assembly, House. "SC Infantry Battle Flag of the Confederate States of America Act of 2015." Act 90, 121st Session, adopted July 14, 2015. https://www.scstatehouse.gov.

South Carolina House of Representatives. *Bipartisan Campaign Reform Act of 2001*. Committee on House Administration. 107th Cong., 1st Sess. H. Rept. 131, pt. 1. Library of Congress. Washington, D.C.: Government Printing Office, 2001.

"South Carolina News." *Yorkville (SC) Enquirer*, February 20, 1879.

"South Carolina News." *Yorkville (SC) Enquirer*, May 13, 1892.

South Carolina Picture Project. "Hamburg Massacre," 2015. https://www.scpictureproject.org.

"The South Carolina Rail-Road and the Augusta Bridge." *Edgefield (SC) Advertiser*, February 19, 1852.

South Carolina Supreme Court. *Reports of Cases Heard and Determined by the Supreme Court of South Carolina*. Vol. 9. N.p.: R.L. Bryan, 1879.

"The Southern Campaign: Daybreak in North Carolina." *New York Times*, October 14, 1878.

Southern Enterprise. Greenville, South Carolina, March 18, 1868, 1.
"Sparnick Trial." *Courier-Journal*, Aiken, SC, May 27, 1876.
"A Specimen Carolina." *Daily Phoenix*, Columbia, South Carolina, March 12, 1871.
"State News." *Queen Bee*, Denver, CO, December 2, 1886.
"State News: Aiken, Sep. 3." *Newberry (SC) Herald*, September 12, 1877.
Stone, Williams. *Attorney General Stone's Report of the Hamburgh Massacre*. July 12, 1876.
"A Story About Hamburg S.C." *Aiken (SC) Recorder*, June 19, 1891.
"The Struggle of '76." *Abbeville (SC) Press & Banner*, September 29, 1909.
T.R.G. "Fury of the Floods: Augusta Submerged by the Raging Savannah." *Edgefield (SC) Advertiser*, September 20, 1888.
"Tax Assessor's Notice." *Edgefield (SC) Advertiser*, September 21, 1864.
Taylor, Bill. Interview by Michael Smith, July 24, 2020.
Taylor, Rosser H. "Hamburg: An Experiment in Town Promotion." *North Carolina Historical Review* 11, no. 1 (January 1934): 20. North Carolina Archives and History.
"Terrible Havoc Feared from Floods." *Abbeville (SC) Press & Banner*, September 2, 1908.
"Terrible Loss: Augusta and Hamburg Under Water." *Journal and Review*, Aiken, SC, August 28, 1908.
"The Thanks of Edgefield Due Gov. Scott." *Edgefield (SC) Advertiser*, June 1, 1871.
Thomas, Bobby. North Augusta City Council meeting, public input. North Augusta, SC, June 15, 2020.
Thomson, Alexander McDonald. "The Election of Angus Cameron." *A Political History of Wisconsin*. Milwaukee, WI: C.N. Casper Company, 1902.
"Threatened Trouble in Georgia." *Yorkville (SC) Enquirer*, August 26, 1875.
Tilson, Misty A. *Augusta: Surviving Disaster*. Charleston, SC: Arcadia Publishing, 2002.
"To Horse! To Horse!" *Edgefield (SC) Advertiser*, August 7, 1861.
Toole, Gasper L. "90 Years in Aiken County." *Aiken (SC) Standard and Review*, March 31, 1959, 2.
Town Council of Aiken. "Petition for Increased Power in Collecting Fines and Levying Taxes, Also Describing a Recent Fire." South Carolina Department of Archives and History, November 25, 1839.
Trinkley, Michael, et al. *Cultural Resources Survey of the North Augusta Riverfront Project, Aiken County, South Carolina*. Chicora Foundation Inc., provided by City of North Augusta, July 1, 2004.
"Trip to Augusta." *Edgefield (SC) Advertiser*, January 12, 853.
"The Trouble at Ridge Springs." *Abbeville (SC) Press and Banner*, August 26, 1874.
"The Troubles in Edgefield." *Abbeville (SC) Press and Banner*, September 30, 1874.
"The Truth About Hamburg." *Anderson (SC) Intelligencer*, August 24, 1876.

"Two Generals." *Weekly Constitutionalist*, Augusta, Georgia, September 1, 1875.
U.S. Congress. "Butler, Andrew Pickens." *Biographical Directory of the United States Congress* http://bioguide.congress.gov.
———. "Butler, Matthew Calbraith." *Biographical Directory of the United States Congress*. http://bioguide.congress.gov.
U.S. Department of the Treasury. "Financial Panic of 1873." https://bit.ly/2QqbB9W.
U.S. Geological Survey. *South Carolina Floods and Droughts, 1893–2002*. https://www2.usgs.gov.
U.S. House of Representatives. "The Massacre of Six Colored Citizens." Washington, D.C., July 18, 1876, 2.
U.S. Senate. *South Carolina in 1876: Testimony as to the Denial of the Elective Franchise in South Carolina at the Elections of 1875 and 1876*. 44th Cong., 2nd Sess. Misc. doc. 48, vols. 1–3. Washington: Government Printing Office, 1877.
Underwood, James L. *Deadly Censorship: Murder, Honor & Freedom of the Press*. Columbia: University of South Carolina Press, 2013.
"Unveil Monument to McKie Meriwether." *Edgefield (SC) Advertiser*, January 12, 1916.
Uptown, Municipal Association of South Carolina. "Home Rule: Turning Point for Local Governments." June 2012.
"Very Warlike." *Camden (SC) Confederate*, November 30, 1864.
"War on Hamburg." *Daily Phoenix*, Columbia, SC, March 14, 1871.
Wayt, Howard. "Railroad Tracks Belonging to the South Carolina Canal and Railroad Company, c. 1839–1852." *Journal of the Society for Industrial Archaeology* 42, no. 1 (2018).
"What Bloodhounds Can Do." *Anderson (SC) Intelligencer*, October 23, 1879.
"Who Blames Them?" *Edgefield (SC) Advertiser*, January 25, 1865.
Williams, John. Untitled article. *Daily Phoenix*, Columbia, South Carolina, March 17, 1871, 2.
WRDW. "Timeline of Project Jackson: From Beginning to Now." North Augusta, SC, October 18, 2016. https://www.wrdw.com.
Young, Thomas. Interview by Michael Smith, July 25, 2020.

Index

About the Author

A resident of Aiken, South Carolina, Michael S. Smith worked as a journalist in South Carolina for more than twenty years and as a technical writer for the past three years. He has won dozens of South Carolina Press Association awards for writing and investigative journalism, including Journalist of the Year in 2006 and 2008. Smith graduated from Coastal Carolina University in Conway, South Carolina, in 1999 with bachelor's degrees in secondary education and history.